THE LUCENT LIBRARY OF SCIENCE AND TECHNOLOGY

Virtual Reality

by Lisa Yount

LUCENT BOOKS

An imprint of Thomson Gale, a part of The Thomson Corporation

THOMSON
GALE

Detroit • New York • San Francisco • San Diego • New Haven, Conn. • Waterville, Maine • London • Munich

For Harry
who taught me about virtual worlds and gives me the best reality imaginable.

© 2005 Thomson Gale, a part of the Thomson Corporation.

Thomson and Star Logo are trademarks and Gale and Lucent Books are registered trademarks used herein under license.

For more information, contact
Lucent Books
27500 Drake Rd.
Farmington Hills, MI 48331-3535
Or you can visit our Internet site at http://www.gale.com

3 9082 10219 0611

LIBRARY OF CONGRESS CATALOGING-IN-PUBLICATION DATA

Yount, Lisa.
   Virtual reality / Lisa Yount.
      p. cm. — (The Lucent library of science and technology)
   Includes bibliographical references and index.
   ISBN 1-59018-107-7 (hardcover : alk. paper)
   1. Virtual reality—Juvenile literature. I. Title. II. Series.
   QA76.9.V5Y68 2004
   006.8—dc22

                                             2004010682

Printed in the United States of America

Table of Contents

Foreword

"The world has changed far more in the past 100 years than in any other century in history. The reason is not political or economic, but technological—technologies that flowed directly from advances in basic science."

— Stephen Hawking, "A Brief History of Relativity," *Time*, 2000

The twentieth-century scientific and technological revolution that British physicist Stephen Hawking describes in the above quote has transformed virtually every aspect of human life at an unprecedented pace. Inventions unimaginable a century ago have not only become commonplace but are now considered necessities of daily life. As science historian James Burke writes, "We live surrounded by objects and systems that we take for granted, but which profoundly affect the way we behave, think, work, play, and in general conduct our lives."

For example, in just one hundred years, transportation systems have dramatically changed. In 1900 the first gasoline-powered motorcar had just been introduced, and only 144 miles of U.S. roads were hard-surfaced. Horse-drawn trolleys still filled the streets of American cities. The airplane had yet to be invented. Today 217 million vehicles speed along 4 million miles of U.S. roads. Humans have flown to the moon and commercial aircraft are capable of transporting passengers across the Atlantic Ocean in less than three hours.

The transformation of communications has been just as dramatic. In 1900 most Americans lived and worked on farms without electricity or mail delivery. Few people had ever heard a radio or spoken on a telephone. A hundred years later, 98 percent of American homes have telephones and televisions and more than 50 percent have personal computers. Some families even have more than one television and computer, and cell phones are now commonplace, even among the young. Data beamed from communication satellites routinely predict global weather conditions and fiber-optic cable, e-mail, and the Internet have made worldwide telecommunication instantaneous.

Perhaps the most striking measure of scientific and technological change can be seen in medicine and public health. At the beginning of the twentieth century, the average American life span was forty-seven years. By the end of the century the average life span was approaching eighty years, thanks to advances in medicine including the development of vaccines and antibiotics, the discovery of powerful diagnostic tools such as X rays, the life-saving technology of cardiac and neonatal care, and improvements in nutrition and the control of infectious disease.

Rapid change is likely to continue throughout the twenty-first century as science reveals more about physical and biological processes such as global warming, viral replication, and electrical conductivity, and as people apply that new knowledge to personal decisions and government policy. Already, for example, an international treaty calls for immediate reductions in industrial and automobile emissions in response to studies that show a potentially dangerous rise in global temperatures is caused by human activity. Taking an active role in determining the direction of future changes depends on education; people must understand the possible uses of scientific research and the effects of the technology that surrounds them.

The Lucent Books Library of Science and Technology profiles key innovations and discoveries that have transformed the modern world. Each title strives to make a complex scientific discovery, technology, or phenomenon understandable and relevant to the reader. Because scientific discovery is rarely straightforward, each title explains the dead ends, fortunate accidents, and basic scientific methods by which the research into the subject proceeded. And every book examines the practical applications of an invention, branch of science, or scientific principle in industry, public health, and personal life, as well as potential future uses and effects based on ongoing research. Fully documented quotations, annotated bibliographies that include both print and electronic sources, glossaries, indexes, and technical illustrations are among the supplemental features designed to point researchers to further exploration of the subject.

Introduction

Walking onto the Holodeck

As fans of the *Star Trek* TV programs and movies know, crew members of the starship *Enterprise* like to relax by visiting the ship's Holodeck. There they can enter any landscape that their imaginations—or anyone else's—might dream up. They can relive a battle from an ancient war, stand on the swaying deck of a sailing ship tossed by a storm, or have conversations with fictional characters such as Detective Sherlock Holmes.

On the Holodeck, whatever place the crew members choose seems to be all around them. They see it, hear it, feel it, perhaps even taste and smell it. Most exciting of all, they themselves are part of the action. When they walk through a scene, their view of it changes, just as it would if they were walking in a real place. When they speak, characters in the scene answer. When they pick up a rock or a flower, they can see it move and feel its texture and weight in their hands. Yet they know that nothing in the Holodeck scenes is real. It is all created by a computer. As soon as they leave the Holodeck, its imaginary world vanishes and they are back on the starship.

An inventor named Ivan Sutherland imagined something like the Holodeck in 1965. He called it the ultimate display. He pictured it as a room

A student works with virtual reality technology. Ideally, such technology creates virtual worlds where users can manipulate and interact with computer-generated objects.

"within which the computer can control the existence of matter" and can create what he termed "virtual worlds."[1] In the ultimate display, Sutherland wrote, "A chair [that was part of the display] . . . would be good enough to sit in. Handcuffs . . . would be confining, and a bullet would be fatal. With appropriate programming, such a display could literally be the Wonderland into which Alice walked."[2]

Ultimate Displays

The Holodeck and Sutherland's ultimate display have many features in common. In both, computers and related devices turn mathematical information into forms that users can perceive with their senses. People inside the displays feel completely surrounded, or immersed, in these artificial worlds. Objects in the displays look three-dimensional, with different sides of the objects appearing as viewers move around them. The displays are interactive, detecting viewers' movements and changing in response to them, and the changes occur in "real time"—as quickly as they would occur in the real world. In the late 1980s, another inventor, Jaron Lanier, gave such displays the name by which they are still best known: *virtual reality*, often shortened to VR. By that time, the technology needed to create them was already being developed.

Would-be starship travelers today cannot walk onto anything like the *Enterprise*'s Holodeck, nor can they sit in a virtual chair or dodge a virtual bullet in Sutherland's ultimate display. Nonetheless, the technology of virtual reality is starting to become part of people's lives. Players sitting in video arcades or at their home computers or game consoles use features of it to see panoramic, three-dimensional views of real or fantasy scenes. Pilots use more complex VR simulations to practice flying, and construction

A virtual recreation of Los Angeles International Airport allows city planners to test urban renewal ideas and gives police a tool for designing security measures.

an Simulation Team

workers use them to learn how to operate heavy equipment. Surgeons employ virtual reality to plan operations, and psychiatrists harness it to treat some kinds of mental illness. Children in classrooms use VR to tour art and science museums, national parks, or re-created historical events. Scientists use it to see inside the earth or to manipulate molecules and atoms to make new drugs. Designers use it to create new planes, cars, and buildings.

Useful as virtual reality is beginning to be, some experts feel that it raises serious ethical questions. They say it can leave trainees and students with dangerous false impressions and even possibly damage their brains. It can cut people off from face-to-face contacts and make some become addicted to make-believe worlds. Defenders of virtual reality say that these fears are groundless or, at worst, will apply to only a handful of people.

Meanwhile, the time of the Holodeck seems to draw nearer each year as computers' speed and power increase. By the middle of the twenty-first century, many businesses and even homes may have rooms able to create convincing illusions that surround their viewers. If that day comes, virtual reality could change—for better or worse—people's feelings about what is real, what kinds of experience are important, and what it means to be a human being.

Chapter 1

Airplanes to Arcades: The Development of Virtual Reality

Imagine an underground chamber like a cave, with a long entrance open to the daylight and as wide as the cave. In this chamber are men who have been prisoners since they were children, their legs and their necks being so fastened that they can only look straight ahead of them and cannot turn their heads. Some way off, behind and higher up, a fire is burning, and between the fire and the prisoners and above them runs a road, in front of which a curtain-wall has been built, like the screen at puppet shows between the operators and their audience. . . . Our prisoners could [not] see anything . . . except for the shadows thrown by the fire on the wall of the cave opposite them.[3]

The ancient Greek philosopher Plato wrote these words about twenty-four hundred years ago. He used the striking image of the prisoners in the cave to illustrate his belief that what human beings thought of as real objects were merely poor imitations of "ideal" forms that could only be imagined. (In his metaphor, humans were the prisoners, and the shadows on the cave wall were the false reality that they perceived.) But, except for the idea that viewers were held in their cave by force, he could just as well have been describing people experiencing virtual reality. To these people, too, a shadowy, make-believe world can seem real.

Showing the Third Dimension

The pictures on the walls of today's VR "caves" are created by computers, not by flickering flames. Attempts to make imagined visions seem real, though, are far older than computers. Indeed, they may have started in actual caves more than fifteen thousand years ago. Stone Age artists covered the walls of caves at such sites as Lascaux, France, and Altamira, Spain, with vividly colored drawings of bison, reindeer, and other animals. Some archaeologists believe that, perhaps as part of religious rituals, viewers were led into these caves in darkness, following winding paths deep within the earth. When candles or torches were lit, the animals on the cave walls would have seemed to leap out of the blackness. The viewers might well have believed that they had entered a spirit world.

As time went on, artists found many ways to imitate or re-create reality. Beginning in Greece around Plato's time, painters of scenes used as backdrops in theaters suggested a third dimension of depth or distance by showing supposedly faraway objects as smaller than near ones and making lines that in reality would have been parallel (those marking the sides of a road, for instance) come together at a point. A few centuries later, artists in the Roman Empire used similar tricks when they decorated walls in the homes of wealthy citizens with views of sunny gardens and orchards.

In the nineteenth century, inventors found a different way to suggest the third dimension, by drawing on the fact that humans perceive depth by combining images received by their right and left eyes, which are several inches apart and therefore view a subject from slightly different angles. Perhaps the first invention to use this new technique was the stereoscope, which a British man named Charles Wheatstone created in 1833. It used two small drawings of the same scene that had been made from slightly different positions. The drawings were mounted on the sides of a wooden frame that the viewer held in front of his or her face. Mirrors in the center of the framework reflected the pictures into the viewer's eyes. When the frame was adjusted to the right distance, the viewer's brain combined the two images into a single one that looked three-dimensional. Later inventors improved the stereoscope, and it became very popular in homes of the late nineteenth and early twentieth centuries. By then, the paired images used in the device were photographs rather than drawings.

A German teacher named Wilhelm Rollmann used a somewhat different technique to create pairs of images that blended into one three-dimensional picture. Beginning around 1853, he made one drawing

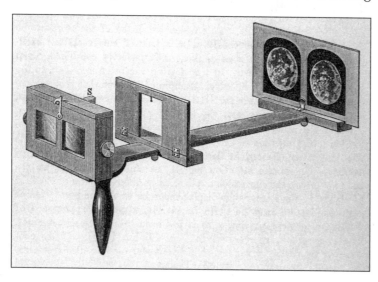

Invented in 1833, the stereoscope allowed viewers to see a drawing or photo in virtual 3-D.

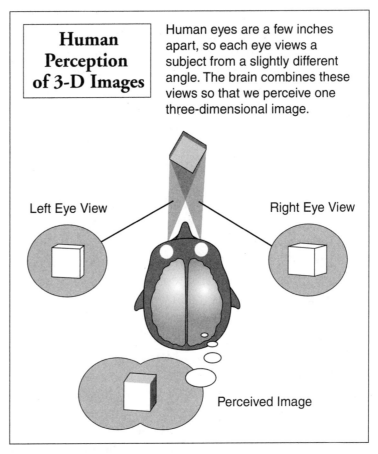

Human Perception of 3-D Images

Human eyes are a few inches apart, so each eye views a subject from a slightly different angle. The brain combines these views so that we perceive one three-dimensional image.

Left Eye View

Right Eye View

Perceived Image

of each pair in green ink and the other in red. The drawings were placed in a stereoscope-like device so that one eye saw the green image and the other the red one. Some filmmakers in the early 1950s adapted Rollmann's approach to create movies that provided at least some illusion of a third dimension. Viewers watched the movies through cardboard-framed glasses with transparent plastic lenses, one tinted red and the other green. When seen through these glasses, the movies' overlapping red and green images formed a single picture that seemed to pop out of the screen. This way of making films was expensive, though, and the illusion of three dimensions was not very convincing. The fad for 3-D movies therefore soon died out.

Morton Heilig, an American inventor, took the 3-D concept even further in an amusement park ride he created around 1960, which he called Sensorama. The rider sat in a movable bucket seat and looked into a periscopelike viewer with a small 3-D movie screen. The viewer also contained stereo speakers, fans, and a device that sprayed out liquids with different smells. When watching a Sensorama movie that showed a motorcycle trip through a city, riders felt the vibrations and turns of traveling over potholed pavements, heard traffic passing by, felt wind in their faces, and smelled food odors from nearby restaurants. Heilig's ride was a crude attempt to create the feeling of immersion, appealing to all the senses, that later virtual reality would also seek. Technology was not yet ready to support him, however. His Sensorama machines were unreliable, and few were sold.

"Flying" on the Ground

Meanwhile, other researchers and organizations were creating illusions for more serious purposes. Commercial flying had begun to develop in the late 1920s, producing a great need for pilots, but training pilots in the air risked both expensive machinery and the lives of the student pilots and their instructors. Around 1930, therefore, Edwin Link, once a maker of pipe organs and player pianos, invented a way for pilots to take some of their flight training on the ground. His "Link trainers" consisted of a mock-up of the controls in a plane, mounted on a platform that changed its angle when the student pilot on the platform moved the controls. Unlike Heilig's Sensorama rides, Link's trainers were interactive: their users' actions affected the display. Interactivity would prove to be as important a part of virtual reality as the feeling of immersion that Heilig tried to create.

The army and navy quickly adapted Link's trainers to teach military pilots. By the early 1940s, when

Link trainers used movies and interactive controls to create virtual flying conditions for these World War II pilots.

thousands of pilots had to be trained quickly to fight in World War II, the military services had added projection of films taken in actual airplanes to the trainers to make the imitation, or simulation, of flight more realistic. Video replaced film in the late 1940s, about the same time a third essential element of virtual reality—computers—began to develop.

Calculating Monsters

In the last year of World War II, the navy used the first electric computer, the Harvard Mark I, to calculate the paths of artillery shells and missiles. The army hoped to do the same with ENIAC (Electronic Numerical Integrator and Calculator), an electronic computer invented by John Mauchly and J. Prosper Eckert of the University of Pennsylvania, but by the time ENIAC was finished in 1946, the war had ended. ENIAC contained thousands of vacuum tubes, something like light bulbs, attached to huge circuit boards. Patterns of vacuum tubes stood for numbers, and ENIAC calculated by turning tubes on and off to change the patterns.

Large businesses began to buy some of ENIAC's descendants a few years later. These early commercial computers filled whole rooms. They were extremely expensive, hard to use, likely to break down, and had far less computing power than the cheapest handheld units today. Nonetheless, compared to humans or even the Mark I, they performed their calculations with amazing speed. After their vacuum tubes were replaced by more dependable devices called transistors in the early 1960s, computers slowly became smaller, cheaper, and more reliable. More businesses and universities began to use them.

Meanwhile, the military also continued to use computers. In the 1950s, the Lincoln Laboratory, a computer research center at the Massachusetts Institute of Technology (MIT), developed a military computer program called the Semi-Automatic Ground Environment, or SAGE. Intended to warn of a possible bomber or missile attack from the Soviet Union, SAGE fed data from numerous radar stations into computers. The computers analyzed the data and put it into a form that could guide interceptor planes to targets that the radar detected.

Unlike other computer programs of the time, which showed their results on punched cards or paper printouts, SAGE displayed its information on video screens. The information appeared in real time, almost as fast as the radar stations gathered the data on which it was based. Few other computers of the era could, or needed to, update their displays so quickly. A third advance was that SAGE operators selected targets for further attention by using a light pen, which interacted with chemicals called phosphors on the inside of the video screens to send electronic signals to the computer. All three of these features later became common to computers in general and were particularly important in virtual reality.

The Sword of Damocles

A graduate student named Ivan Sutherland joined the Lincoln Laboratory in 1960. Three years later he completed a program called Sketchpad, which, like

SAGE, used a video screen and a light pen. A user of Sketchpad could draw lines by touching the screen with the pen and then modify them by typing instructions on a keyboard. The program also let users enlarge or reduce their drawings, save them, and reproduce them. Most of these features had never appeared in a computer program before. Sutherland's invention was the start of computer graphics, an essential part of virtual reality.

Sutherland's inventiveness by no means stopped with Sketchpad. In 1965 he wrote an essay called "The Ultimate Display," in which he described an ideal computer system that allowed users to manipulate "objects" made from data, changing their shape and position on a screen, just as people can move physical objects in the real world. He predicted that scientists would use such displays to test theories in ways that they could never do in reality.

Sutherland realized that the technology to create his ultimate display did not yet exist, but he thought he could make a simpler device that would have some of its features. In 1966, supported by the Department of Defense, which hoped that his invention could be used in improved flight trainers, he began building what he called the Sword of Damocles. He took the name from an ancient Greek legend that told of a king who forced a courtier to eat a meal while seated under a sword suspended above his head by a single hair. Like the mythical sword, Sutherland's creation, a bulky helmet that covered a wearer's entire head, was suspended from the ceiling, though a sturdy metal rod took the place of the hair. The helmet could be turned, but its wearer, like the courtier, had to remain in more or less the same spot.

A set of glass prisms in Sutherland's helmet reflected images from two small video monitors into the helmet wearer's eyes. A computer supplied the images to the monitors. As in the old stereoscopes, each

MIT's Ivan Sutherland demonstrates his Sketchpad computerized drawing program in 1963. He predicted the advent of virtual reality.

monitor showed a slightly different view of the same object, which the wearer's brain combined into a single three-dimensional picture. Unlike the stereoscope images, however, the pictures in the monitors changed when the viewer moved his or her head to look in a different direction. Sensors in the rod and helmet detected the head movement and passed information about it to the computer, which altered the display. In other words, like Link's pilot trainers, Sutherland's helmet was interactive. The Sword of Damocles was the first head-mounted display (HMD), which became one of the two chief kinds of devices through which people experience virtual reality.

Gloves and Helmets

In the early 1970s, Frederick Brooks and others at the University of North Carolina (UNC), Chapel Hill, added the element of touch to HMDs. The Sword of Damocles had included a control wand that a wearer could use to "move" objects shown on the computer screens, but Brooks's team carried this idea further. They developed a handgrip called GROPE-II, which contained tiny motors that pushed back against, or resisted, users' hand movements, a process called force feedback. The resistance could be adjusted, and variations in it created the sensation that a person was handling actual objects. UNC chemists used GROPE-II and its 1980s successor, GROPE-III, to gain the sensation of moving molecules, discovering which ones could be fitted together to make new substances.

Scientists sponsored the development of GROPE-II, but the military and the commercial airlines paid for most of the research on simulation devices. Both were looking for better flight simulators to train pilots to use planes that grew more complicated every year. The cockpits of the newest aircraft included heads-up displays, which projected information about altitude, speed, and so on at eye level

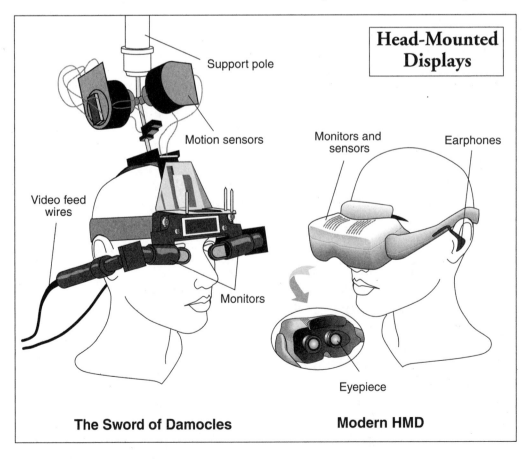

Head-Mounted Displays

Support pole

Motion sensors

Monitors and sensors

Earphones

Video feed wires

Monitors

Eyepiece

The Sword of Damocles   **Modern HMD**

in a form that pilots could see but also see through. These displays meant that during battle, for instance, military pilots did not have to take their eyes off enemy aircraft and look down to obtain this information.

Working at Wright-Patterson Air Force Base in Ohio in the late 1960s, Thomas W. Furness III began trying to incorporate a heads-up display into a pilot's helmet. He wanted to keep the display in front of the pilot's gaze no matter which way the pilot looked. He also hoped to make the display visible against both bright and dark backgrounds. By the early 1970s, Furness's team had created HMDs something like Sutherland's Sword of Damocles. The HMDs included sensors that tracked head position and used computer graphics, which had replaced video in trainer simulations by then.

Furness's group went on to make a helmet that blocked out the real world almost entirely, replacing it with three-dimensional computer graphics. Furness called this system a virtual cockpit, or, more formally, the Visually Coupled Airborne Systems Simulator (VCASS). Completed in 1981, the VCASS helmet was so big and bulky that it reminded people of the one worn by *Star Wars* archvillain Darth Vader. Nonetheless, fighter pilots praised it.

Furness's team went on to build the SuperCockpit, an improved version of VCASS that allowed pilots to see the real world and a virtual display at the same time. Visual and sound systems in the helmet gave the pilot the feeling of being in a three-dimensional environment. Computers generated the environment and could change it according to pilots' actions. Pilots wearing the SuperCockpit could select targets by gazing in particular directions and could fire weapons with voice commands. Force-feedback gloves gave them a sensation of touch when they pressed virtual buttons or triggers displayed in the air in front of them. These features gave the

SuperCockpit, finished in 1986, all the elements of future virtual reality systems. The test model that Furness's group built, however, was the only one ever made. Even the military could not afford to put the SuperCockpit into regular use.

Cheaper and Lighter

The National Aeronautics and Space Administration (NASA) was a government agency, but it had nothing like the military's giant budget. Therefore, when Michael McGreevy, a scientist at NASA's Ames Research Center in Mountain View, California, decided to experiment with simulations in the early 1980s, he knew he had to use technology far less expensive than that in VCASS and the SuperCockpit. Instead of cathode-ray tubes (CRTs) like those used in television sets, he decided to use liquid crystal displays (LCDs), which had recently been developed. These small displays, sold at the time as mini-TV sets, did not produce pictures as sharp as those in VCASS's CRTs, and unlike those in VCASS they did not show color—but they cost only a few hundred dollars each. McGreevy's team incorporated two of these displays into a mask, along with wide-angle lenses and position sensors, to create a device he called VIVED (Virtual Visual Environment Display) in 1984. The mask had the great advantages of being lightweight and costing a mere two thousand dollars instead of VCASS's $1 million. However, it also had a major drawback: It was not interactive.

By this time, computers had become so small, cheap, and reliable that most businesses had one. Ordinary people were even beginning to use them in their homes. Professionals in a number of fields, including art and entertainment as well as science and education, started experimenting with ways to make computer displays imitate reality. Among them were the developers of video games, which had come into existence about a decade earlier. Thomas Zimmerman and

Jaron Lanier, working at first for the video game company Atari and later on their own, developed a glove that contained magnetic position trackers and optical fiber sensors that could tell a computer both where a wearer's hand moved and how the fingers bent. The computer altered its displays accordingly. They began selling their DataGlove, as they called it, about the time Furness's SuperCockpit was completed.

Scott Fisher, a programmer who had gone from Atari to McGreevy's team at NASA, decided to combine the two groups' technologies. He bought a DataGlove

Liquid Crystal Displays

LCD Construction

Liquid Crystal Displays (LCDs) are lighter and thinner than Cathode Ray Tube (CRT) displays. This makes them perfect for head-mounted displays.

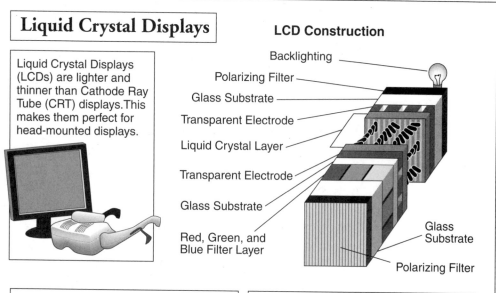

Backlighting
Polarizing Filter
Glass Substrate
Transparent Electrode
Liquid Crystal Layer
Transparent Electrode
Glass Substrate
Red, Green, and Blue Filter Layer
Glass Substrate
Polarizing Filter

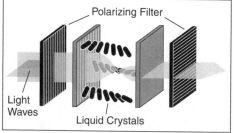

Polarizing Filter
Light Waves
Liquid Crystals

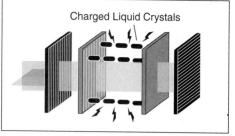

Charged Liquid Crystals

LCDs use polarizing filters to control light. Vertical light waves are allowed through a polarizing filter. A layer of liquid crystals bend the waves to pass horizontally through a second polarizing filter. When electrically charged, the crystals line up and light waves pass through unchanged. When the waves reach the second polarizing filter they cannot pass through.

and, with Zimmerman's help, adapted it to VIVED. He added an improved stereo system that imitated the way sound changes in three dimensions, as well as other technology that let the computer creating the display respond to voice commands. Fisher called the complete combination VIEW, or Virtual Interactive Environment Workstation. Among other things, NASA used it to develop a "virtual wind tunnel" for testing parts of the space shuttle.

VIEW's graphics were primitive, its display blurry, and its tracking system too slow to keep up with a user's movements well. Still, it was inexpensive, fairly comfortable to wear and use, and freed users from direct attachment to the computer. Best of all, it created a feeling of what Fisher called telepresence—the impression that its user was actually inside the virtual environment. "Thus," writes virtual reality pioneer Mark Pesce, "was virtual reality born."[4]

Virtual Reality's Boom and Bust

The term *virtual reality* did not yet exist, however. Jaron Lanier coined it in the late 1980s to describe a new system he called RB2, or "Reality Built for Two," which would allow two users to share a computer-generated environment. Lanier stressed in a 2002 interview that he had been "interested in having more than one person at a time in [the] computer-generated world, so that those people could see each other and share the world as a means of communication. To me, the term 'world' refers to what's out there outside of you, but the term 'reality' refers to what you share with other people . . . [and] have to interact with."[5] Although several other terms with more or less the same meaning as virtual reality, including *artificial reality*, *virtual worlds*, and *immersive computing*, were created and are sometimes still used, Lanier's term has remained most popular.

Media stories about virtual reality began appearing everywhere in the early 1990s. Video gamers and fans of fantasy games such as *Dungeons and Dragons*™ hoped that this new technology would make the games more thrilling than ever. Scientists and engineers looked forward to studying and manipulating virtual objects, ranging from houses and cars to molecules, in ways that had never been possible before. Businesspeople dreamed of instant wealth as they set up companies to manufacture virtual reality hardware and software. To all these groups, and an excited public as well, Ivan Sutherland's ultimate display seemed just around the corner.

Virtual reality devices, however, remained bulky, expensive, and unreliable, and the computers of the day lacked the speed and power to make VR illusions really convincing. When the true state of virtual reality technology became obvious, people lost interest in the field, and many companies and organizations devoted to it went bankrupt. As late as 2000, VR pioneer Frederick Brooks complained that the technology still "barely worked."[6] In the first years of the new century, however, advances in computers and VR devices have begun to stir excitement about virtual reality once again.

Computer engineer Jaron Lanier coined the term virtual reality, *which he believed best signified the idea of a shared experience.*

Chapter 2

Goggles, Gloves, and CAVEs: The Technology of Virtual Reality

If viewers could look inside *Star Trek's* Holodeck, they would probably find advanced versions of the same kinds of equipment and software that virtual reality systems contain today. The heart of the system would surely be a powerful computer with programs that produce complex, three-dimensional images. Devices would send information from the computer to most or all of the crew members' senses: sight, hearing, touch, and probably smell and even taste. Other devices would pick up information about the members' body and hand movements, voices, and perhaps even thoughts, and would convey this information to the computer.

Drawing Virtual Pictures

The best virtual reality systems—the ones owned by large universities and corporations—use expensive supercomputers with special graphics capability, such as the Silicon Graphics Onyx series. Many home computers can create more limited versions of virtual reality with software such as QuickTime VR. Video game consoles like the Sony PlayStation 2 and Microsoft Xbox, which are a form of computer, also produce convincing three-dimensional graphics, stereo sound, and sometimes limited touch sensations as well. Neither they nor home computers, however, create the feeling of being completely immersed in a virtual world that systems with large screens can produce.

A computer that creates virtual reality needs tremendous processing power because the work it must do is so challenging. First, the computer must draw, or render, complex, realistic-looking graphics. Software usually builds these graphics from combinations of polygons, which are two-dimensional geometric shapes with three or more straight sides.

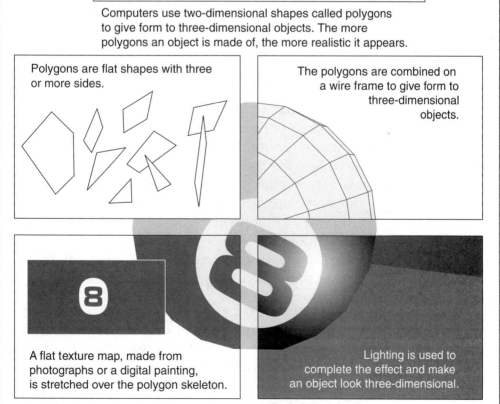

Three-Dimensional Computer Graphics

Computers use two-dimensional shapes called polygons to give form to three-dimensional objects. The more polygons an object is made of, the more realistic it appears.

Polygons are flat shapes with three or more sides.

The polygons are combined on a wire frame to give form to three-dimensional objects.

A flat texture map, made from photographs or a digital painting, is stretched over the polygon skeleton.

Lighting is used to complete the effect and make an object look three-dimensional.

Polygons are even used to make curved shapes (which consist of many small polygons attached at very small angles) because computers can draw polygons much more easily than they can draw free-form shapes. The more polygons an image contains, the more realistic it will look, and the longer it will take to draw. A single landscape may contain thousands of polygons.

The computer graphics software and processor combine the polygons into frames or skeletons that look as if they are made out of wire, then add textures and colors. Instead of drawing the textures a bit at a time, programs often use texture "maps" made from photographs of real materials or objects, such as rocks. They overlay the maps on the frames as if covering them with wallpaper. Shading and lighting effects complete the illusion of three dimensions.

Rendering a detailed, three-dimensional picture even once is hard enough. A computer used for virtual reality, however, must do this task over and over—between twenty and thirty times a second—because the display on a computer monitor constantly fades out and must be restimulated, or refreshed. A person's eye holds the impression of an image for about a tenth of a second, so the screen must be refreshed more often than this or else it will seem to flicker. (For the same reason, film moves through a movie projector at a speed of thirty frames a second so that people will see motion rather than a "slide show" of still photos.) In reproducing a complex picture thirty times, a computer has to draw tens of millions of polygons each second.

Communicating with Users

A computer running a virtual reality system also must change its display when users turn their heads or move their hands—and must do so without a delay that the users can notice. If there is a lag, people using the program may feel disoriented or even suffer simulator sickness, a reaction much like seasickness or airsickness. People have sensors in their inner ears, bones, muscles, joints, and skin that help their bodies maintain balance and keep track of their position. If these sensors receive conflicting information, or information that disagrees with what the eyes seem to be seeing, the person is likely to feel dizzy and nauseated. This can happen when the head turns and the view of a virtual landscape changes more slowly than the person would expect the view of a real landscape to change. It can also happen when a person's body senses that it is standing still, yet the surroundings seem to be moving.

The computer receives information about the user's actions from sensors or trackers attached to the head, hands, or other parts of the body. These sensors detect movement by measuring changes in a magnetic field, ultrasound waves, or light-emitting or reflecting material. Sensors on the head, mounted in a helmet or a pair of glasses or goggles, tell the computer the direction in which the user is looking. Sensors in gloves tell how much the fingers bend and where they point. Sensors on the body show how the user moves within a room. Sensors in tools such as wands, three-dimensional mice, and force balls (ball-shaped devices, mounted on a platform, which can be pushed, pulled, or twisted in place to move a cursor in three dimensions) let the user select an object in the virtual display and tell the computer how and where to move it. The most elaborate sensors reveal movement in all of what are called the six degrees of freedom: movement along three axes (left-right, or X axis; up-down, or Y axis; and forward-backward, or Z axis) and three forms of twisting around each axis (roll, pitch, and yaw).

The computer, in turn, sends information to the user's senses. It most often communicates with vision through special glasses. With some virtual reality programs, including those that run on home

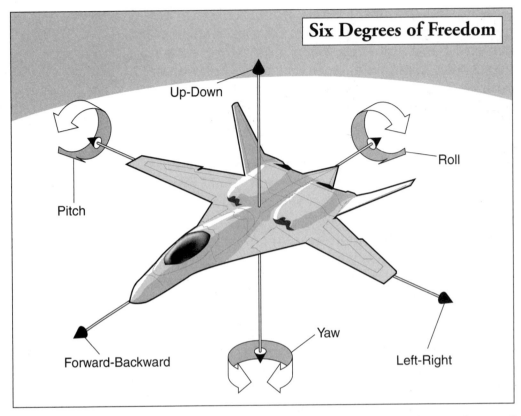

Six Degrees of Freedom

Up-Down

Roll

Pitch

Forward-Backward

Yaw

Left-Right

computers, users wear glasses that are descendants of the old cardboard-and-plastic ones given to audiences watching 3-D movies in the 1950s. The two lenses in these glasses are either different colors or contain filters that line up light waves in different directions, or polarities. The computer monitor showing the VR program, like the old 3-D movie screens, shows overlapping images in the two colors or polarities, and the brain combines them.

Another type of VR glasses, called shutter glasses, were first developed in the 1980s. The lenses of these glasses are liquid-crystal displays that can be made either clear or opaque by changes in electric current. The monitor screen switches rapidly between left-eye and right-eye views of objects or scenes, and impulses from the computer clear and darken the lenses at the same rate, usually thirty to sixty times a second. As a result, the left eye always sees one view and the right eye sees the other. As with other stereoscopic vision devices, the brain combines the two images into a single one that appears three-dimensional. A beam of infrared light passing between the computer display and the glasses synchronizes the two. Shutter glasses are probably the most common way of showing 3-D visual effects today. Some companies sell inexpensive shutter glasses that work with home computers.

Sound, Touch, and Smell

The computer in a virtual reality system uses sound as well as vision to create the illusion of a three-dimensional environment. Like the eyes, a person's two ears receive slightly different messages because they have different positions on the head. The brain uses differences in the timing, loudness, and pitch of sounds to locate objects in space. Room-sized VR systems send messages to the ears through two or more stereophonic speakers in different parts of the room. Systems featuring head-mounted displays use tiny speakers in the HMD's helmet. The computer changes the signals coming through these speakers to reflect the user's movements. For instance, if a user turns away from a rushing river in a virtual display, the computer will make the sound of the water seem to move from the front to the side of the user's head.

Many virtual reality systems include gloves or other devices that convey a sense of touch. These tools are called *haptic*, from a Greek word meaning "touch." Force feedback, which uses motors to provide resistance to hand movements, is the most common way of transmitting touch sensations. Some home VR and video game systems use force feedback, for example, to suggest the resistance and vibration of the steering wheel when the user drives a virtual racing car.

A penlike, or stylus, device called Phantom, which is often part of the virtual reality design systems that some businesses use, employs force feedback in a more complex way. For instance, when two people using Phantoms in different locations are linked by a computer network, the stylus can make one person's finger follow a path traced by the other.

In elaborate VR systems, a computer can transmit touch sensations to a whole hand or arm by means of a framework or exoskeleton. One device of this kind is called CyberGrasp. CyberGrasp's exoskeleton fits over a glove that contains twenty flexible sensors. These sensors pick up complex data about the hand's motion and send it to the computer. The computer translates the information into a picture of a virtual hand making the same motions and shows the hand on its monitor. At the same time, it sends signals to motors that roll or unroll cables in different parts of the framework. The cables push or pull the parts of the framework, thereby conveying sensation to the fingers. In June 2001, *Time International* reporter Adi Ignatius described using CyberGrasp:

> On a computer screen a 3-D image of a ball appears as well as a representation of my hand, which I control by moving the big, spiderlike exoskeleton I'm wearing. As I manipulate the ball, the fingertips of the CyberGrasp sense the force feedback via a network of artificial tendons. I 'feel' the ball as I bat it through cyberspace. There are flaws: the hand sometimes goes through the object. But it's a thrill touching something that isn't there.[7]

A few experimental systems have even added smell to virtual reality displays. One called iSmell mixes chemicals from a "scent cartridge" to produce smells ranging from cotton candy to ocean breezes, much as painters can mix, say, yellow and blue pig-

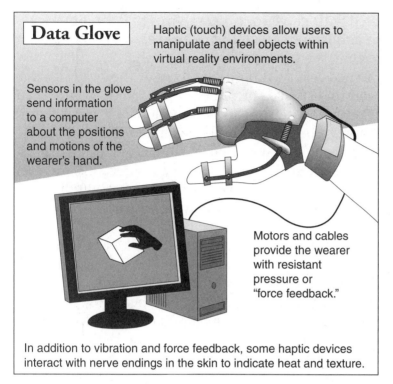

Data Glove

Haptic (touch) devices allow users to manipulate and feel objects within virtual reality environments.

Sensors in the glove send information to a computer about the positions and motions of the wearer's hand.

Motors and cables provide the wearer with resistant pressure or "force feedback."

In addition to vibration and force feedback, some haptic devices interact with nerve endings in the skin to indicate heat and texture.

ments together to make green. So far, however, smell-producing technology has not been very convincing, and there has been little demand for it. Inventors have not even tried (yet) to put taste sensations into virtual reality.

Head-Mounted Displays

Two main types of virtual reality systems are used today. One type, descended from pilot-trainer helmets and Ivan Sutherland's Sword of Damocles, features a head-mounted display. HMDs are far less bulky now than they were in virtual reality's early days, although some still cause neck and back pain if worn too long. HMDs that use cathode-ray tube screens provide some of the most convincing virtual reality displays, but they are expensive. Displays using liquid crystals, descendants of Michael McGreevy's VIVED and Scott Fisher's VIEW, are less costly, but they are also less sharp and clear. HMDs are often used with gloves or other devices that send messages to and from parts of the body other than the head.

One type of HMD delivers what is called augmented reality. A modified form of the heads-up displays developed for pilots in the 1960s, augmented reality headsets use combinations of prisms and lenses to reflect computer-generated images into the user's eyes in a way that makes the semitransparent images seem to float above real objects. A surgeon wearing this kind of headset, for instance, might see an X-ray or an ultrasound image of part of a patient's body placed over a view of the actual patient. Instead of being distracted by having to look back and forth between the patient and a monitor showing the image, the surgeon can see both at the same time. One problem with augmented reality headsets, however, is that their displays can be hard to read in bright light, just as the tiny LCD screens on digital cameras are often hard to see on a sunny day. Today, most augmented reality systems are still experimental, but they are beginning to be tested for commercial use.

CAVEs

Around 1990, Thomas DeFanti, then a researcher at the Electronic Visualization Laboratory at the University of Illinois at Chicago, got the idea for the second main type of virtual reality system while trying on a suit in front of a triple mirror in a clothing store's dressing room. Looking at the three reflected images of himself, he pictured a system that would place multiple images on the walls and even perhaps the floor and the ceiling of a small room, creating a virtual environment that completely surrounded its viewers. (Ivan Sutherland, too, had imagined that his ultimate display would fill a room.) DeFanti, Carolina Cruz-Neira, and Daniel Sandin built the first room-sized virtual reality system in 1991. Recalling the metaphor that Plato had used long ago, they called it the Cave Automatic Virtual Environment, or CAVE.

The first CAVE was a cube-shaped room measuring ten feet on each side. Rear projection units showed pictures on three of its four walls, and an overhead projector placed another image on the floor. "Unlike users of the video-arcade [head-mounted display] type of virtual reality system," Sandin and DeFanti wrote, "CAVE 'dwellers' do not need to wear helmets, which would limit their view of and mobility in the real world."[8] Instead, people in the CAVE wore lightweight shutter glasses, which an infrared beam synchronized with the changing computer display. The glasses contained tracking sensors that told the computer where the wearers were standing and where they were looking. The people moved objects in the display with control wands.

The CAVE proved so appealing that researchers and inventors created many variations of it. These CAVE-type systems immerse their users in the virtual experience more completely than any other kind of VR environment. (Some CAVEs have ripped projection screens because people have been so convinced by the systems' illusion that they literally walked into the room's walls.) They let people move naturally within the environment, freed from

Thomas DeFanti (left) and Daniel Sandin pose in their CAVE in 1998. CAVEs are the second chief type of virtual reality system.

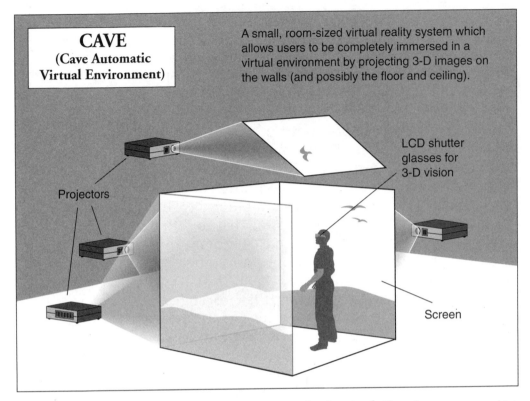

CAVE
(Cave Automatic
Virtual Environment)

A small, room-sized virtual reality system which allows users to be completely immersed in a virtual environment by projecting 3-D images on the walls (and possibly the floor and ceiling).

LCD shutter glasses for 3-D vision

Projectors

Screen

bulky equipment and physical ties to a computer. Perhaps most important for the scientists and engineers who use them, they allow several people to share the same VR experience. This means that, say, engineers, marketing executives, investors, and others can come together to examine and modify a virtual model of a car or a plane. Of all existing virtual reality systems, CAVE-type systems come closest to *Star Trek*'s Holodeck.

The main drawback of CAVEs is that they are very expensive. A complete CAVE system can cost a million dollars or more. As a result, only a few large universities and wealthy corporations have them. In the hope of bringing CAVE-type systems to more people, inventors have created simpler and less costly versions that have some of the same advantages. One, the PlatoCAVE, projects an image on only one wall. Another form, the RAVE (Reconfigurable Advanced

Visualization Environment), can be taken apart and moved to different locations. It has three eight- to ten-foot screens that may be used separately or combined in various ways.

The group who invented the CAVE also created a smaller version, which they call the ImmersaDesk. The ImmersaDesk is the size of a large desk or drafting table and contains a single large screen. When a viewer wearing shutter glasses faces the desk, he or she sees a three-dimensional image that appears to rise above the desk.

Beyond HMDs and CAVEs

A new type of VR system, sometimes called artificial reality, combines some features of both HMD and CAVE displays. It blends live action with computer graphics. In one such system, called LiveActor, the user wears a suit containing thirty sensors that pick up the motion of different parts of the body. As the user moves in a CAVE-like room about ten feet by twenty feet, the computer makes a character in the projected virtual environment carry out the same actions. Artificial reality has been used to create artworks in which viewers in effect become part of the display. It has also let users "participate" in sports ranging from boxing to golf, either for training purposes or just for fun.

Convincing as the best VR systems can be, most observers agree that virtual reality technology has a long way to go before it can produce displays as good as those on the Holodeck. VR devices are often unreliable and uncomfortable to use. Stand-alone VR systems also are still very expensive: according to CyberEdge Information Services, which reports regularly on the industry, the average price of such a system worldwide was about $142,000 in 2002. Nonetheless, more and more people in education, science, industry, business, and entertainment are finding new and exciting uses for virtual reality.

Chapter 3

The Virtual Classroom: Virtual Reality in Training and Education

Parents often complain that their children spend too much time playing video games, but some army leaders say they should not be in such a hurry to gripe. Three-dimensional video games are proving to be an ideal tool for training soldiers. Cadets at the famous military academy at West Point, in New York, for instance, train with a tank simulation game called *Steel Beasts*, adapted from a commercial game of the same name. Similarly, the Marine Corps has modified the popular *Doom*, making the game's monsters into enemy soldiers. The army makes a highly accurate military simulation game named *America's Army* available for free downloading from a Web site as a recruiting tool. According to an article published by the Australian Academy of Science, "The skills learn[ed] by playing interactive computer games . . . the ability to process information rapidly and to solve problems interactively . . . might just make . . . the ideal military commander of the future."[9]

Simulations for Soldiers

Video games are not the only military training tools that use virtual reality. The U.S. armed forces spends about $4 billion a year on training equipment and programs involving simulations, and many of these feature some degree of VR. Simulations help soldiers learn how to use complex equipment, work together, and rehearse missions. They let commanders plan battles and try out different combat tactics, maneuvering platoons of virtual soldiers, vehicles, and weapons over thousands of square miles of terrain. "The shift from live range training to computer-based training is fundamentally changing the way we prepare our soldiers for the future,"[10] says W.H. ("Dell") Lunceford Jr., director of the Army Model and Simulation Office in Arlington, Virginia. A task force of the U.S. Defense Science Board concluded in a report in 2000 that low U.S. casualties in military actions in the 1990s was due in large part to the use of simulators in training and planning.

Virtual reality games like America's Army *(pictured) can be helpful military training and recruiting tools.*

Military groups sometimes work with universities and private companies to develop training simulations. The army, for instance, joined with the University of Southern California to create the Institute for Creative Technologies (ITC), where experts from the university, the movie industry, and the military invent games and simulations that help soldiers and officers learn to make decisions in a battle zone. In an August 2002 article in *Business Week*, Arlene Weintraub described one vivid ITC simulation:

> In a war-ravaged village, an Army lieutenant sets off on a spy mission. As he navigates a dank tunnel on his way to the enemy's hideout, rats scurry around his feet and bats flutter overhead. The bone-jarring rumble of a passing enemy vehicle shakes rocks loose from the bloodstained walls. Watchdogs soon spot him and bark furiously, causing his heart to race.[11]

Military forces in other countries also train soldiers and officers with virtual reality. For instance, Australia's Commonwealth Defence Science and Technology Organisation used a simulation to help pilots learn how to fly a new type of helicopter. The simulation featured an accurate virtual landscape, created from aerial and satellite photos, which included buildings, roads, trees, and "even virtual kangaroos that bounded away on hearing the helicopters approaching."[12]

Fliers, Drivers, and Miners

Virtual reality began as a training tool for pilots, and flight simulators are still among the most popular virtual reality training programs. Whether designed for military or commercial pilots, flight simulators greatly reduce the amount of time a pilot must spend in the air during training. They therefore cut down on both expense and risk. Critics warn that

simulators can never completely replace actual flight experience because, for instance, they cannot show all the things that can happen to a plane in bad weather. Some types of aircraft, especially helicopters, are also hard to simulate accurately. Still, even relatively simple simulator programs that run on home computers have proved very useful in training pilots. A navy study found that student pilots who used Microsoft's Flight Simulator program were 54 percent more likely to obtain above-average scores in real flight tests than pilots who had trained without the program.

Like the military and the air industry, large businesses are starting to see VR as the best way to teach workers how to do jobs that are complex, dangerous, or both. VR training programs are not yet widespread because they are expensive to develop, but they can save companies money in the long run by cutting down on the amount of costly real equipment, such as heavy machinery, that must be used in training. Simulation programs also reduce risk to machines, the environment, and even human lives. Finally, the computers that run the programs can be set up to keep records of the students' actions, giving teachers, students, and researchers an opportunity for review that live training cannot offer.

Commercial pilots today train on virtual reality flight simulators like this one. Simulation reduces the risks and time of actual training.

Some companies use driving simulators in much the same way that airlines use flight simulators. These simulators are too expensive for ordinary driver training, but corporations such as Amoco (American Oil Company) employ them to teach truck drivers to handle icy roads and other hazards. Some drivers of police cars, fire trucks, and ambulances also use simulators to learn how to travel safely at high speeds.

Virtual reality is also being used or tested as a training tool for other hazardous jobs. Fifth Dimension Technologies in Santa Clara, California, for instance, has developed simulators that teach people to use hauling trucks, electric shovels, and other machines in mines. One of their programs, the Integrated Virtual Mine, connects simulators representing different kinds of machines so that trainees can learn to work as a team.

An inventor demonstrates a simulation program designed to train engine mechanics. Simulators provide safe yet realistic training conditions.

Similarly, some railroads train engine drivers and other workers with simulators. For example, a classroom VR program called RealityManager teaches groups of rail employees how to evacuate underground stations, run equipment manually if auto-

matic systems fail, and deal with angry passengers. It presents simulated situations to which the employees respond, taking on the roles of characters in each situation. The instructor discusses their reactions, pausing or replaying the scenarios as needed.

Virtual Bodies and Minds

Doctors, ranging from future physicians still in medical school to experienced surgeons, also increasingly do part of their learning in virtual reality. Rather than studying anatomy (the structure of the body) by cutting up corpses of animals or of people who have donated their bodies to science, students at some medical schools now use virtual reality programs based on pictures from CT (computerized tomography), MRI (magnetic resonance imaging), and other medical imaging technology. The programs let the students see organs and body parts in three dimensions, examine them from any angle, and make virtual cuts into or even "fly through" them. They can repeat the process as often as they need to, whereas a real dead body can be dissected only once.

Some of the best anatomy programs owe their existence partly to a convicted murderer. They are based on the National Library of Medicine's Visible Human project, which used X-ray scans, CT scans, and MRI scans to make three-dimensional maps of real male and female bodies. The male body belonged to Joseph Paul Jernigan, who donated it to science before he was executed for his crimes in 1993.

Other VR programs let medical students and nurses practice opening veins to draw blood or inserting tubes called catheters into body openings before they ever touch a living patient. Force-feedback gloves such as CyberGrasp give the students a literal "feel" for the textures of different tissues and the amount of resistance a surgeon would meet while cutting into them. Experienced surgeons also use VR to learn and to practice complex techniques for operating on the heart and the brain. Studies have shown that training with simulators improves surgeons' skill in carrying out real operations.

Some psychiatrists are using virtual reality to learn more about the bizarre worlds inside their patients' minds. A five-minute program called "The Bus Ride," demonstrated at American Psychiatric Association conventions in 2002 and 2003, shows an ordinary public transit trip as it might appear to a person with schizophrenia, a severe mental illness. The program, presented on a wraparound video screen inside a simulated bus, is based on reports from real people with schizophrenia and psychiatrists who have treated them. It features distorting hallucinations and voices that exist only in the patient's imagination. "It can help doctors understand what a patient goes through,"[13] says Daniel Frey, who has the illness.

Even some people who like to play sports are training with virtual reality. Canadian inventor Don Wilson has created what he calls the Virtually Perfect Golf Learning System, in which a golfer wears a pair of 3-D glasses and stands in the center of a triangle of video cameras. A screen, viewed through the glasses, shows the golfer his or her own body with an "ideal golfer" superimposed on it. This figure looks more like a skeleton made of wire than like Tiger Woods, but it is effective at showing the student golfer how he or she should be standing and moving. The golfer learns by moving along with the ideal figure in slow motion. After trying the program, a golfer named Robbie Weisz reported: "I could see everything in a new way. I noticed that the pro [the idealized figure] was holding his wrist hinged much further down than I was. A swing [with a golf club] happens so fast—maybe a second. In a regular lesson, you can commit so many errors and not even realize it. But with this, you can visualize it perfectly."[14]

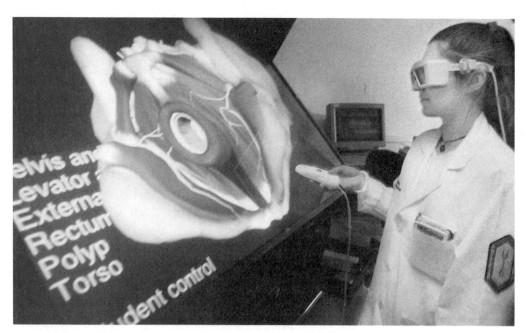

Virtual reality can be a special help in educating and training people who cannot read, say executives at the Naledi 3D Factory, a South African company that develops VR education and training programs for groups including UNESCO (UN Educational, Scientific, and Cultural Organization). Naledi's programs have covered such subjects as cleanliness and good health habits, prevention of HIV infection and AIDS, and techniques for generating electric power. "A picture paints a thousand words," says the company's Web site. "An interactive 3D model paints millions!"[15]

VR programs now train medical students in anatomy and surgery, and can even help psychiatrists enter the world of the mentally ill.

VR in the Classroom

In the United States and other developed countries, virtual reality is entering young people's classrooms as well. A 1997 report to the National Science Foundation stated that "VR improves learning . . . by providing the learners with new, direct experiences of phenomena they could not have experienced before, either in direct interaction with the real world or using other technologies."[16]

Virtual reality is one of many forms of computer technology that schools have begun to use often in the last decade. The U.S. Department of Education reported in late 2003 that about 90 percent of people aged five to seventeen use computers, mostly at school but also in libraries or at home. Students gather information from the World Wide Web for reports or use e-mail and chat rooms to work on projects with other students in distant parts of the country or the world. Sometimes they post the finished projects on Web sites of their own. Some students take complete classes online from "virtual schools."

Schools can seldom afford fully immersive virtual reality, but they often use programs that at least provide three-dimensional graphics and interactivity. These programs run on standard computers. Some require free downloadable programs or inexpensive gear such as shutter glasses, but many need no additional software or equipment.

One example of a school virtual reality program is called Touch the Sky—Touch the Universe. It uses an interactive 3-D model of the solar system to help students learn about astronomy. Students fly a virtual spaceship through the model, looking at it from different viewpoints. They watch eclipses and changes of phase as the planets and moons move through their orbits. They can zoom in on individual planets, moons, asteroids, and comets to study them more closely. When they touch a planet or other astronomical object with the mouse pointer, the program shows information about the object, such as its size and the time it takes to complete its orbit. Students can speed up or slow down the movement of the system and find out how these changes affect the movement of particular planets or moons.

Another educational virtual reality program, made by a company called Sunrise VR, teaches architecture "in its [natural] element—earth, sea, and sky."[17] Named Virtual Chicago, this program lets students follow the development of modern architecture by flying over Chicago and exploring more than forty of the city's buildings. The program's developers say they chose Chicago because that city is "a living museum of architecture,"[18] housing the world's first skyscraper and other unusual buildings. The program includes an introduction to architecture throughout history, a description of modern architectural movements and famous architects, examples of different architectural forms and styles, and a demonstration showing how a skyscraper is built.

Do-It-Yourself VR

Students can create their own virtual reality projects with the Virtual Reality Development Lab, a kit of hardware, software, and instructions sold by Digital Technology Frontier in Phoenix, Arizona. They photograph a site with a digital camera included with the lab, then use the lab's computer and software to "stitch" the photos together into panoramas—images that show the site as it would look if a viewer stood inside it and turned in a complete circle. They combine multiple panoramas with audio and links to text or still pictures to develop a VR tour of the site. The tour can be viewed with glasses included in the kit. It can also be posted on the Web to share with other students.

Some VR programs help students with special needs. For instance, a company named Veridian created a program called Virtual Reality Education for Assisted Learning, which helps students with severe hearing impairment learn life skills such as how to cross a street safely. Another program gives disabled students practice in finding their way around schools and other common environments. An experimental program developed in Britain teaches social skills to people with autism, a brain disorder that makes learning how to get along with others difficult.

Students can follow the development of Chicago's skyline using the VR program Virtual Chicago (pictured).

Virtual Tours

Other programs, some available commercially on CDs and others appearing for free on Web sites, let people learn about the world by paying virtual visits to distant places. Many virtual tours feature panoramic views through which a visitor can turn by using a mouse. Some panoramas also allow the viewer to look up and down, as if standing in a cube or a bubble, and to zoom in on particular parts of the panorama. Clicking on certain spots in the panorama may take the viewer to other panoramas, still photos, or text information about those spots.

One Web site of this type, created by Peter Danford, is called the Tibet Game. In addition to providing a panoramic view of Lhasa, the capital of Tibet, the site lets viewers interact with characters on the screen, buy objects such as prayer flags, and give away pictures of the Dalai Lama (Tibet's spiritual leader), with the aim of gaining enough "karma" to "enter nirvana." Danford has also created virtual tours of the Great Wall of China, a Hong Kong voyage, the Shanghai acrobats, and more, and posted them on free sites on the Web.

Tourist boards of cities and countries provide other virtual tours, such as the one of the world-famous opera house in Sydney, Australia. Travel businesses like Disney Cruises also sometimes offer virtual tours of their rooms or the places they visit. Perhaps the most "far out" tour of all is NASA's Virtual Astronaut, a Web site aimed at students in grades five through eight which includes panoramic views of the Space Station and a host of related learning activities.

In addition to tours on Web sites, some art and science museums use virtual reality to educate people who visit them in person. The Hayden Planetarium at the American Museum of Natural History in New York City, for instance, has an on-site show that lets viewers fly through a 3-D representation of thousands of stars. Museum astrophysicist Michael M. Shara calls it "the CAVE gone wild."[19] The simulation, based on data from satellite telescopes, is so accurate that, after the museum closes, Shara and fellow astrophysicist Jarrod R. Hurley use it to test their theories about the movement of star clusters. Watching the stars move on the planetarium dome, they have seen features of the clusters' behavior that they had never noticed when looking at their data on ordinary computer monitors.

Evaluating Educational VR

As with other uses of computers in learning, experts disagree about how useful virtual reality programs for education and training really are. Some praise such programs for extending the range of materials and learning experiences that students can have.

They say that VR makes study material more exciting, so students will be more likely to remember what they learn. Expensive as VR programs are to develop, supporters also claim that creating or buying these programs may be cheaper in the long run than maintaining laboratories in which students do live experiments or letting adult trainees use real machinery.

On the other hand, Edwin J. Delattre, dean of the School of Education and professor of philosophy in the College of Arts and Sciences at Boston University, writes, "Learning how to behave properly in a classroom, a museum, or a library, and acquiring the sense of respect and, at times, of reverence and awe that befits us in such places cannot be accomplished in virtual reality."[20] He and other critics fear that students who rely too much on virtual reality and other computer programs will miss the personal contact and the lessons about social interaction that a face-to-face classroom can teach.

Critics of educational and travel VR programs also say that these programs, no matter how well done, can never have the impact of an actual visit to a museum, park, or historical site. Similarly, people who question the value of VR training programs say that because such programs cannot completely simulate the behavior of machines or people, they cannot be as effective as on-the-job experience. Because virtual reality programs for training and education, like other VR programs, are still fairly limited, even most of their supporters agree that for the foreseeable future, they most likely will—and should—be used as additions to traditional classrooms or standard training methods rather than as replacements for them.

Chapter 4

Custom-Made Worlds: Virtual Reality in Science and Business

M eteorologists (scientists who study weather and climate) would like to step into a hurricane to find out how the winds inside it behave—and come back out alive. Chemists and drug designers would like to examine the shape of complex molecules and build new ones, atom by atom. Paleontologists (scientists who study ancient forms of life) would like to travel back in time to see how dinosaurs walked. Since doing those things in real life is difficult or impossible, some of these scientists are doing them in virtual reality instead.

Many people think of virtual reality as little more than a high-tech toy, but a growing number of scientists, physicians, engineers, industrial designers, and businesspeople are coming to see it as a serious tool. It brings people in different countries together without the bother of a plane ride and lets them look at cars and buildings that have not yet been constructed.

51

With the help of robots, it may soon let surgeons operate on patients in distant cities and astronomers "walk" on the surface of Mars. It turns equations, graphs, and other abstract data into forms that people can see and touch. As Ivan Sutherland wrote decades ago, it lets them "gain familiarity with concepts not realizable in the physical world. It is a looking glass into a mathematical wonderland."[21]

Molecules and Jets

One of the first VR systems to include a sense of touch, GROPE-II at the University of North Carolina, Chapel Hill, was designed to help chemists create new compounds by working with three-dimensional models of molecules. Electrical forces make a molecule attract some kinds of molecules and repel others. Touch sensors gave the chemists the sensation that molecules were sliding together if they were attracted or pushing away from each other if they were repelled. Today, improved programs at the same university let chemists see and feel individual atoms.

NASA used another early virtual reality system, VIEW, to create a virtual wind tunnel to help engineers and designers analyze the effects of air flow on planes and the newly developed space shuttle in the 1980s. More recently, the same agency's Glenn Research Center in Cleveland, Ohio, has employed a variation of the CAVE system, which they call the GRUVE (Glenn Reconfigurable User-interface and Virtual reality Exploration), to improve jet engines. "It's very difficult to understand the complex turbulent flow of hot gases in a jet engine," says Jay Horowitz, manager of the GRUVE laboratory. "Virtual reality lets [scientists] . . . immerse themselves in the hot flowing gases of the jet. They can make a change in the [engine] and then see how that change affects the fluid dynamics in the hot gas flow. This is critical for designing more efficient engines which produce less pollutants."[22]

The Virtual Underground

Geologists working for some energy companies use virtual reality to help them find deposits of oil and natural gas. Their customized VR programs transform huge masses of data into three-dimensional images of underground formations and earthquake faults. The geologists can turn the images, zoom in on areas that they want to study more closely, and make slices through the virtual formations at different angles.

Shell Oil and Phillips Petroleum are two of the companies that employ virtual reality in this way. Designers working for Phillips created the conCAVE, a modified CAVE with a large, curved wall screen, a dome-shaped top, and a flat bottom, all of which can show images. Viewers can move a geological feature from one part of the display to another in order to study it in different ways. The floor view, for instance, is best at showing the direction in which a feature slants because it shows a flat, maplike view of an area. The wall views work better to reveal a feature's thickness because they are more three-dimensional.

Shell geologists navigate through their 3-D maps with a CubicMouse, a cube-shaped tool with three rods representing axes of length, width, and depth. By sliding and turning the rods, a viewer can make slices through a map in any direction. The rods can be locked into position so that people can pass the mouse around without altering the slice. Laurent Bourdon, a principle seismic interpreter for Shell, says that virtual reality and the CubicMouse became "immediately useful in reducing the time that it takes us to explore new drilling sites and to re-evaluate [oil and gas] reservoirs following several years of production."[23] The tools cut the time needed to plan the path of new wells by half and speeded up the overall design of the wells by 10 to 20 percent, Bourdon claims.

Dinosaurs and Ancient Cities

"Hard" sciences such as chemistry and geology are not the only ones that employ virtual reality. Some archaeologists use VR programs to re-create ancient buildings and cities. Brown University in Providence, Rhode Island, for instance, has developed a virtual reality program based on its archaeologists' discoveries about the city of Petra, which flourished about twenty-five hundred to two thousand years ago in what is now Jordan. Brown researchers use the VR system to visualize the structure of Petra's Great Temple, map the layout of the city, and see all the locations where particular types of finds, such as pottery, have been made. By combining all the architectural details and objects so far discovered into a life-size model of the temple, the VR program both serves as a record of the archaeology team's work and helps to bring the ancient site to life. Scientists at Brown are developing additional programs to help them make three-dimensional reconstructions of objects such as bowls from the fragments that they find at the site.

Biologists as well as physical scientists are experimenting with virtual reality. For example, Alexie A. Sharov, an entomologist (a scientist who studies insects) at Virginia Polytechnical and State University in Blacksburg, Virginia, has used VR to create life-size, 3-D models of insects such as cockroaches and grasshoppers. "You can even get swallowed by a grasshopper and find yourself in its abdomen,"[24] he says. Similarly, in the late 1990s, paleontologists at the National Museum of Natural History, part of the Smithsonian Institution in Washington, D.C., used a computer to create a 3-D model of one of the museum's dinosaurs based on laser scans of its bones. The model not only helped the scientists improve the museum exhibit but gave them new information about the way the dinosaur probably moved when it was alive.

Virtual Surgery

Virtual reality has found many uses in medicine. One VR tool for surgeons, the DextroScope, lets them use images of patients to plan and experiment with complex surgeries before performing them on the real people. Surgeons in Singapore used the DextroScope in early 2001 to plan an operation to separate twin baby girls from Nepal who were joined at the head, for instance.

Augmented reality helps surgeons perform laparoscopic, or "keyhole", surgery, in which operations are done with small tools inserted into the body through tiny incisions. Because this kind of surgery causes less injury than traditional surgery with large incisions, it helps patients recover more quickly. That, in turn, lowers the cost of medical care because the patients can leave the hospital sooner. The drawback of keyhole surgery, though, is that surgeons can see what they are doing only indirectly, through images on a screen. Augmented reality makes their work easier by projecting CT or MRI scans of the operated area over the actual part being operated on. Surgeons who use

*A virtual image of a
patient's brain
projected onto his
head shows surgeons
where and how to
operate.*

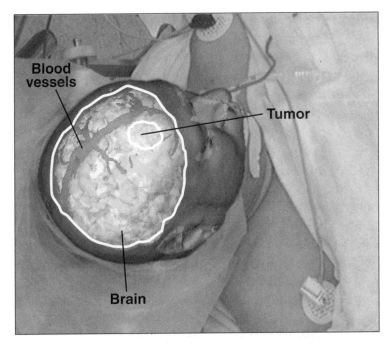

the technique have said that it helps them gain back
some of the three-dimensional vision and feeling
that they had with conventional surgery.

Some virtual or augmented reality systems for surgeons include touch information as well as visual
displays. The surgeon may use this touch sense to
control robot instruments that carry out the actual
operation. Such instruments can make movements
more precise than those of even the best human surgeons. Using a combination of VR displays, force-
feedback touch devices, and robot arms manipulated
by remote control, surgeons have operated on a
beating heart through an opening in the chest that
was smaller than the width of a pencil.

With similar blends of VR and robotics, surgeons
can operate on people many miles away, allowing surgeons to "in essence . . . dissolve time and space,"[25] as
surgeon Urban Geisthoff says. This use of VR is still
experimental, but in the future, such "telesurgery"
might be used to operate on people in locations that
are hard to reach, such as a rain forest, a submarine,

or even a space station. The Department of Defense is looking into the possibility of using telesurgery on soldiers in battle zones.

In one of the most unusual medical uses of the haptic power of virtual reality, "E-touch" software from Novint Technologies in Albuquerque, New Mexico, combines touch sensors with three-dimensional ultrasound to let expectant parents have the sensation of touching their baby while it is still in the womb. Tom Anderson, head of Novint, says that the sensation is "a little bit squishy . . . similar to skin. You can feel along the surface [of the unborn baby, as translated from the ultrasound images] and feel a little bit of pressure and contour."[26]

Fighting Fears

Some medical uses of virtual reality depend on programs that do not sound very appealing. One features a kitchen full of spiders. Another pictures a mountainside with a sheer drop to a valley far below. People use these programs in a psychiatrist's office, learning to overcome powerful fears called phobias. About 10 percent of people in the United States suffer from phobias such as fear of flying, fear of heights (acrophobia), and fear of spiders (arachnophobia). When these phobias are severe, they can keep people from holding a job or even leaving their homes.

Psychiatrists normally treat phobias by carefully exposing people to the things they fear, first in small amounts and then in larger ones, until they get used to them. A person who is afraid of spiders, for instance, might learn to play with a fuzzy toy spider, then watch a spider in a glass box, and finally be exposed to an uncaged spider. This process, called desensitization therapy, cures phobias or reduces them to manageable levels in at least three-quarters of the people treated. Arranging desensitization experiences, however, can be expensive, impractical, or even unsafe.

Furthermore, when a person is exposed to an actual frightening situation, no one knows exactly what will happen. Patients may resist the treatment because they are afraid of losing control. Virtual reality can provide a solution to these problems.

Computer scientist Larry Hodges of the Georgia Institute of Technology and psychiatrist Barbara Rothbaum of Emory University in Atlanta made the first controlled study of virtual reality treatment for phobias in 1995. One of their programs treated people who were afraid of heights. It showed a virtual imitation of a glass-walled elevator, such as some expensive hotels have. Patients first saw a hotel lobby as it would appear if the elevator were on the ground floor. They then saw the lobby from one floor up, then two floors, and so on until the view showed the lobby from eight or nine stories up. Hodges and Rothbaum also tested a program that treated fear of

Larry Hodges (right) demonstrates his VR program for desensitizing people to things they fear. The program has proved highly effective.

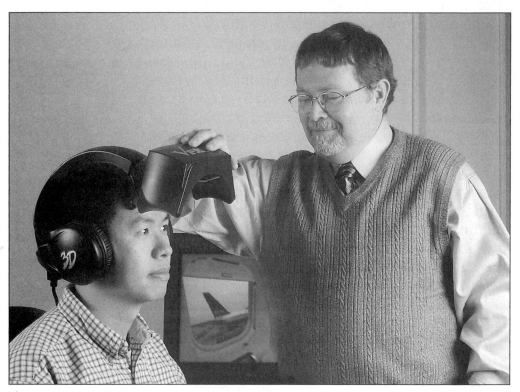

flying. Their study showed that the virtual reality treatments were just as effective as live desensitization therapy.

A number of psychiatrists and patients who have tried virtual reality phobia therapy say they like it better than the real thing. The chief reason is probably that both know the VR scenario is completely under the therapist's control. In a program to treat fear of public speaking, for instance, the therapist can make a virtual audience sit quietly, applaud, or yell and scream. This control means that the experience is never more frightening than the patient can stand. It can also be stopped at any time. Experiencing a frightening situation in virtual reality seems to make a good intermediate step between simply talking about it and facing it in the real world. Patients who refuse live desensitization therapy often accept the VR version.

Most VR phobia programs use head-mounted displays. Some involve other equipment as well. One program to treat fear of flying, for instance, includes a vibrating chair that imitates the motion of a plane and a sound system that mimics the noise of aircraft engines. Partly because of the equipment they require, VR phobia treatments can be expensive, and only a few psychiatrists have them. The treatments also give some patients simulator sickness or add to their difficulty in separating fantasy from reality. As technology improves, however, VR treatments for phobia are likely to become more common.

Virtual reality has been used to treat other mental conditions as well. One is posttraumatic stress disorder, which caused many soldiers who served in the Vietnam War in the late 1960s and early 1970s, for example, to suffer later from nightmares and flashbacks of terrifying experiences. A program called Virtual Vietnam lets such soldiers relive stressful situations, including flying a helicopter and walking through a jungle clearing, until they become desensitized to them and are better able to control their anxiety. Other VR programs treat vertigo (dizziness), eating disorders, cigarette addiction, and sexual problems. Programs that several people can use at the same time work well for group therapy, helping group members build a sense of community through their shared experiences.

Virtual reality scenarios can also help psychiatrists evaluate different kinds of brain function, such as memory, planning, and coordination. For example, children thought to have attention deficit disorder, which makes sitting still and concentrating difficult, can be tested in Virtual Classroom, a simulation of a schoolroom. The teacher in the simulation gives the child various assignments, such as working math problems. Meanwhile, the child hears noises and sees distracting events both inside and outside the classroom. (The child sees the outside distractions through a virtual window that looks onto a school playground.) The therapist measures how well the child carries out the teacher's assignments as the amount of distraction increases.

Controlling Boredom and Pain

People with physical problems use virtual reality, too. Patients whose brains have been injured by accidents or by strokes must repeatedly exercise certain muscles, such as those in their hands, in order to gain back full control of them. People with other injuries need different kinds of exercise, such as riding on stationary bicycles. Patients often become bored with these exercises and may refuse to continue them. They find, however, that pedaling a bicycle is more interesting when they watch a VR program that gives them the illusion of riding through a beautiful meadow, a redwood forest, or a mountain trail. Similarly, doing hand exercises becomes more fun when the user, wearing VR gloves, is chasing fluttering butterflies or playing a virtual piano.

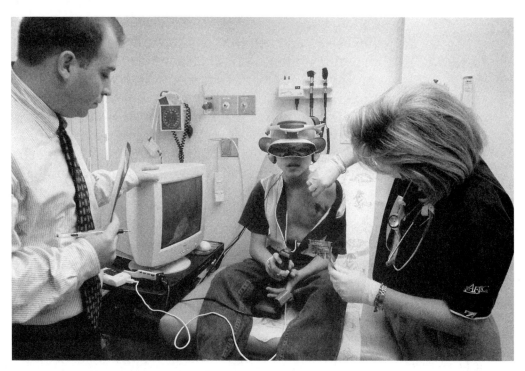

The distractions of virtual reality can do more than keep people from being bored; they can block actual pain. One VR program helps burn victims, who must undergo painful skin scraping every day. The program takes the patients on exciting adventures such as a deep-sea dive, a roller-coaster ride, or a trip to a ski resort. Using it "was like watching a movie," one burned teenager said. "I got totally absorbed in my virtual world and forgot about the pain."[27] Other experimental programs have distracted people receiving different kinds of painful treatment, such as dental operations.

A young patient diverts his attention away from a painful medical treatment by becoming absorbed in a virtual reality program.

Designing with Virtual Reality

Engineers planning a plane or a car or architects designing a building traditionally begin with two-dimensional drawings, or blueprints, and then proceed to three-dimensional work using computer-aided design (CAD) programs. They then usually build a clay mock-up and finally a complete, full-size model, called a prototype, for further testing. Prototypes, however, can cost up to a million dollars apiece, and new ones must be built if design problems are uncovered. A number of major car and plane manufacturers, architects, and other industrial designers, therefore, now save hundreds of hours and millions of dollars by building their prototypes in virtual reality before they make real ones. "If you can get it right the first time, it will mean a massive cost saving,"[28] says Nick Matthews, principal research fellow at the Warwick Manufacturing Group, a British firm that helps businesses find uses for new technology.

VR prototypes help engineers because they can be examined from all angles, including some that would be difficult or impossible to see on a real prototype. With some VR systems, designers can even touch the virtual prototypes. They can also see how the prototypes will function. They can test plane designs in virtual wind tunnels, for instance. Viewers of virtual models of buildings can "walk" through them, noticing how the spaces inside relate to each

An architect constructs a virtual building. This process allows architects to spot mistakes before starting work on the real project.

other. Sometimes they also see how a building relates to other nearby buildings or landmarks such as parks or plazas.

VR prototypes are handy to show to visiting executives, financial supporters, or potential customers as well. Groups can study them together, try out different possibilities, and look for problems that were not obvious in drawings. When flaws are detected, the designs can be changed immediately. In one early architectural use of VR, for instance, reviewers discovered that a wall that the architects proposed to build between the lobby and the hallway of a new building made the hallway too narrow. Because the problem was uncovered before the structure was actually built, it could be corrected easily.

Systems for building virtual prototypes are expensive, so only large companies use them today. They may become more widespread, however, as costs drop and businesses realize how quickly they can pay for themselves. A CAVE system costs about four hundred thousand dollars, for instance, but a single complete physical prototype for a car may cost two hundred thousand dollars. The CAVE, therefore, can earn back its cost when it eliminates the building of only two physical prototypes.

Cars and Buildings

Several European auto companies, including the makers of Jaguar Formula One racing cars, employ virtual reality to design their vehicles. Mercedes-Benz uses its VR center in Stuttgart, Germany, not only for designing but for crash testing. Studies have shown that results from these simulated crashes match the results from crash tests of real cars 98 percent of the time. The virtual testing saves money because it does not require expensive material to be destroyed. The computer also shows what happens to each part of the car, including parts that might not be visible or easily studied in a real crash test.

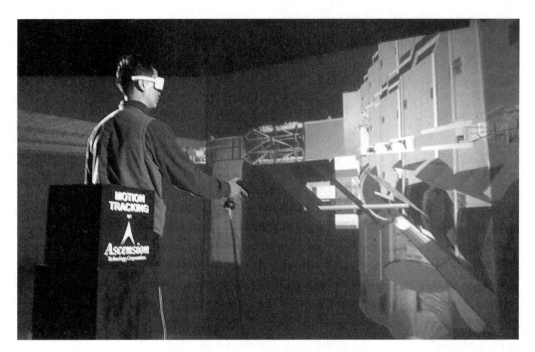

A NASA engineer helps design a space station in virtual reality. Making virtual prototypes helps engineers get projects right the first time.

The Beck Group, an industrial architecture company in Dallas, has developed a VR design program that it calls DESTINI (Design Estimating Integration Initiative). Potential customers using this program first choose a general type of building from among several models. They then specify the size and number of floors they want and the types of materials they would like to use. In just a few minutes, the program turns these specifications into a three-dimensional model of a building. The customers and company architects can modify the model in various ways, trying out many possibilities. When they agree on a final model, the program generates CAD drawings, a list of materials, a cost estimate, a time line for construction, and an estimate of the amount of energy needed to heat and light the building. Beck officials say that DESTINI has reduced the time between their first meeting with a customer and the beginning of construction by up to 40 percent.

Other architects use virtual reality to show customers mock-ups of model homes. "By bringing the floor plans to life, buyers get a better understanding of what it would be like to actually live in this house," says Mitchell C. Hochberg, president and CEO of Spectrum Skanska, a builder of luxury homes in the Northeast. Such virtual tours are far cheaper to prepare than actual model homes, Hochberg points out. Hochberg calls the VR tours "our single most important marketing tool."[29]

Long-Distance Meetings and Virtual Stores

Businesses use virtual reality for many purposes besides design. Executives in some large corporations with many branches set up virtual conference rooms for meetings, gaining most of the advantages of face-to-face communication without the expense and stress of long-distance travel. VR pioneer Jaron Lanier thinks that as computers and Internet communication grow more powerful, this type of technology will eventually develop into what he calls tele-immersion, which will convince conference participants in different locations that they really are in the same room.

Companies such as PepsiCo, the maker of Pepsi Cola, use VR to plan and test displays of their products in supermarkets and convenience stores. Other businesses put limited forms of VR, chiefly panoramic 3-D graphics, on their Web sites. The Las Vegas Hilton and another Las Vegas hotel, the MGM Grand, offer Web viewers 360-degree views of their hotel rooms, for instance. Ford's and Toyota's Web sites include 3-D pictures of their cars, trucks, and SUVs. Some businesses even imagine a day when whole stores will appear on the Internet, complete with 3-D aisle displays and virtual clerks who call customers by name, remember their previous orders, answer questions, and suggest additional products that the customers might want to try. For some retailers, virtual stores may replace brick-and-mortar ones entirely.

Chapter 5

Arcades to Avatars: Virtual Reality in Art and Entertainment

A viewer floats through a mysterious, semitransparent landscape, like a diver underwater. Breathing in, the person rises through the bare branches of a huge tree. As the person enters the branches, their empty twigs suddenly become covered with leaves. The viewer then breathes out and drifts down, down, into the rocky soil on which the tree stands. Now the viewer gazes upward into the tree's roots.

This was the experience of people who entered a room containing an art installation called *Osmose*, a French word meaning "flows through." *Osmose*, designed by Canadian artist Char Davies and first exhibited in 1995, is one of many examples of art that uses virtual reality. Viewers of *Osmose* wore head-mounted displays as well as devices, invented by Davies, that fitted around their chests and sensed their breathing. The chest sensors sent messages to the computer controlling the exhibit. Responding to this information, the computer changed the display in ways that made the viewers seem to rise and fall.

Immersive Art

Beginning with the Stone Age cave painters of France and Spain, artists have always tried to immerse viewers in their imagined worlds. It is no wonder, then, that modern artists have been attracted to virtual reality since its start. One of the first people to create works using computerized simulations that viewers could walk into was Myron Krueger, who was a computer scientist as well as an artist. Starting in 1969, he constructed several projects that he called artificial reality.

In a Krueger project named *Glowflow*, sensors in the floor of a darkened room detected viewers' movements, and a computer changed lights and sounds in the room in response. Another of Krueger's installations, *Videoplace*, could be set up in several locations at the same time. Computers in the different spots were linked by telephone. This networking let the movements of a viewer in one location affect what someone in the other location experienced.

Char Davies's virtual artwork Osmose *lets viewers interact with a tree from roots to branches. VR art allows all the senses to experience the work.*

Tree Pond. Digital frame captured in real-time through HMD (head-mounted display) during live performance of immersive virtual environment *Osmose* (1995). Courtesy Char Davies (www.immersence.com).

Videoplace thus was an ancestor of teleconferencing as well as an artwork. Krueger said later that it "created a place that consisted of the information we [the viewers in the two locations] both shared."[30]

Another American artist, Lynn Hershman, created a different kind of virtual reality with an interactive videodisc called *Lorna*, which she displayed in 1982. The program on the disc began by showing a frightened-looking, middle-aged woman watching television in a dingy hotel room. Viewers could control the woman's behavior by clicking on the television and other objects in her room. Each click selected a section of the disc showing a different action. As a result, each person who visited the installation saw a different version of Lorna's story. Depending on viewers' choices, Lorna might eventually overcome her fears and leave her room for good, destroy the television, or, alternatively, kill herself.

As virtual reality improved in the late 1980s and 1990s, artists continued to explore it. The technology had its own exhibition, *Virtual Reality: An Emerging Medium*, at the Guggenheim Museum in New York City in 1993. One work presented there, created by Jenny Holzer and Jeff Donovan, was called *Bosnia*. It showed viewers a patterned landscape of brilliant orange earth and blue sky flecked with clouds. Clusters of cinderblock huts dotted the scene. When a viewer selected a hut, a recorded voice began telling a story about the war that was then destroying Bosnia's land and people. Each hut held a different voice and story.

Artists still like to play with virtual reality. For instance, Canadian inventors Vincent John Vincent and Francis MacDougall created software that let viewers take part in Vincent's virtual reality art installations. Stereo cameras in the installations photographed viewers' movements, and the software integrated them into the virtual reality programs as video images. Viewers then saw themselves, in real time, chasing and capturing virtual butterflies, composing music on virtual instruments, or painting designs on a virtual canvas. Vincent's installations appeared in more than six hundred places around the world in the early 2000s, including the Smithsonian Institution and the Canadian World Expo pavilion.

Making a Statement

French artist Maurice Benayoun used a CAVE installation to make a political comment in *Far Near (E-motion)*, which he exhibited in 2001 and 2002. In this artwork, two people in the CAVE, working back-to-back, "dug" toward one another by making virtual holes in stacks of still images facing them on the screen. Each digger's goal was to find the image of the other person. The diggers could talk to each other by means of microphones. Benayoun wrote that the signals controlling the sound and images

> follow[ed] a random path around the planet via [the] Internet, through war zones, places marked by pollution, poverty, and . . . communication saturation. . . . When the Internet signal passed through one of these troubled zones, the communication between the two diggers [was] affected. [The] picture [was] altered, distorted according to the nature of the attack. . . . The sound [was] also disrupted when the signal [went] through these "zones." . . . The sound distortion . . . [was] composed of pre-recorded sounds [and] real time sounds from radios serving the disrupted zones, thus creating a type of sound matrix.[31]

The Birth of Video and Computer Games

Only a few people have a chance to visit a virtual reality art exhibit. Far more will meet VR technology in a video arcade or at the controls of a home computer or a game console. Video and computer games cannot immerse people as completely as a CAVE, but they are certainly interactive, and most use the best 3-D graphics and stereo sound that they can afford. Some games provide sensations of touch and vibration as well. Video and computer games thus can be considered to be a type of virtual reality. Indeed, because these games are so popular, many experts think that if virtual reality ever does become widespread, it will probably do so first in the form of such games. (Surveys have shown that people in the United States spend about $10 billion a year on video games, consoles, and electronic toys—more than they spend on movies.)

The virtual reality–style video and computer games of today have three ancestors: computer games, video games, and fantasy role-playing games. All three developed together in the 1970s and 1980s.

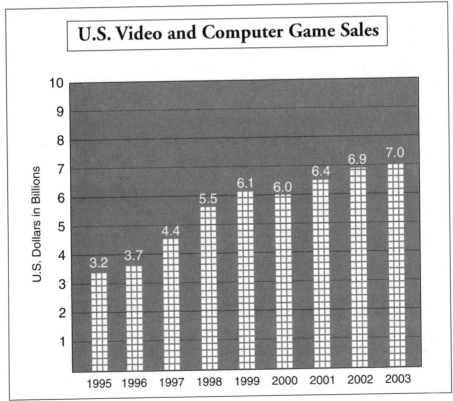

U.S. Video and Computer Game Sales

U.S. Dollars in Billions

1995: 3.2
1996: 3.7
1997: 4.4
1998: 5.5
1999: 6.1
2000: 6.0
2001: 6.4
2002: 6.9
2003: 7.0

Source: Entertainment Software Association (www.theesa.com).

Even in the 1960s, when only large universities and corporations and the military had computers, some people found ways to make the hulking machines play games. Perhaps the first computer game was *Spacewar*, in which players made the computer move two simply drawn rocket ships against a background of stars. Students at MIT created *Spacewar* in 1962, and the game soon spread to other universities through computer networks that predated the Internet.

One fan of *Spacewar* was a University of Utah student named Nolan Bushnell, who managed an arcade at an amusement park in Salt Lake City during his summer vacations. After Bushnell graduated, he began trying to make *Spacewar* into a coin-operated arcade game. He more or less succeeded in 1971, but the game did not sell well.

Meanwhile, Ralph Baer, a German-born inventor, had started work on a game system that could be connected to a television set. In 1971, while Bushnell was peddling his *Spacewar* look-alike to arcades, Baer sold his invention to Magnavox, a company that made televisions and other home entertainment equipment. Magnavox named the device Odyssey and released it a year later. It was the first home video game console. It had two controllers and twelve plug-in circuit boards, each dedicated to a particular ball game (Ping-Pong, volleyball, hockey) or shooting game. The games had very simple black-and-white graphics and no sound effects.

Pong Takes Over

After Nolan Bushnell saw a demonstration of the Odyssey system, he and fellow inventor Ted Dabney formed a company called Atari and set about inventing their own virtual Ping-Pong game, a computerized version in an arcade machine. Their game included the sound of a ball hitting a paddle and took its name, *Pong*, from that sound. The first time

Atari cofounder Nolan Bushnell sits in his workshop. Atari introduced the first programmable home video game system in 1977.

Bushnell tried out his *Pong* machine, in a bar called Andy Capp's in Sunnyvale, California (the heart of the computer-invention hotspot nicknamed Silicon Valley), in 1972, the machine broke down because eager players stuffed it too full of quarters. Atari sold eighty-five hundred machines the following year—something of a record for arcade machines.

In 1974, Atari produced a *Pong* console that could be plugged into a television, much as Baer had envisioned. It, too, became a best seller. (It also led to a lengthy patent battle between Atari and Magnavox.) Atari went on to introduce a programmable video game console for home televisions, called VCS (Video Computer System), in 1977. This meant that one console could be used for multiple games and switched from one to another through software, rather than requiring a separate console or circuit board for each game. Programmable game consoles for televisions became tremendously popular in the early 1980s.

Meanwhile, also in 1974, Atari launched an arcade game called *Tank*, which for the first time included a computer memory chip that held graphics. Armed with such a chip, game consoles could finally begin to have visual displays that went beyond a few cursors and lines on a screen. A Chicago company called Midway introduced *Gun Fight*, the first arcade video game to use a computer microprocessor chip, a year later. The chip allowed the game to have more complex action than earlier ones, including a computerized opponent that moved unpredictably. Computerization was thus leading both arcade and home video games closer to virtual reality.

Do-It-Yourself Adventures

In the early 1970s, when video game machines could do little more than smack balls, fire guns, and direct dueling spaceships, some gamers were focusing on different tools that had no such limits: language and their own imaginations. They used those tools in another type of game, called fantasy role-playing games. One named *Dungeons and Dragons*™ was the most popular.

At first, these games used no machinery at all. Acting the parts of elves, wizards, warriors, and other magical characters, players worked together to make up their own stories. They searched for treasure and fought with monsters in all sorts of fantasy worlds, guided only by complicated rule books and dice that determined the outcome of game events, such as which characters would be wounded in a battle. Some people who liked fantasy role-playing games also liked computers, however, and they soon began trying to make computerized versions of the games. Computer graphics were almost nonexistent at the time, so these early inventors, already used to picturing their adventures in their imagination with the help of words, simply used text on the monitor screen to describe what players were supposed to be experiencing.

Zork, introduced in the late 1970s, became perhaps the best known early text-based adventure game. People played it on large computers at first, but when personal computers began to become common in the 1980s, Marc Blank, one of *Zork*'s creators, joined with Joel Berez to design a version of the game that would run on the smaller machines. By 1987, microcomputers' capabilities had improved enough for one of the game's descendants, called *Beyond Zork*, to contain limited graphics, including a map. This and the many other games created for home computers in the 1980s developed into the computer adventure games of today.

VR Comes to Arcades

Beginning in the early 1990s, the heavy helmets of virtual reality gear joined video games in large amusement arcades. A number of new businesses started to make VR systems for arcades, but the computers of the time could provide only primitive graphics, head-mounted displays and gloves were uncomfortable and sometimes produced simulator sickness, and users sometimes tripped over the cables needed to attach the equipment to computers. When disappointed players stopped spending their money on these setups in the mid-1990s, many of the new companies went bankrupt.

Arcade games often still include aspects of virtual reality, however. Players today can roll virtual bowling balls through three-dimensional landscapes shown on floor-to-ceiling screens, feeling the weight of the balls through force-feedback effectors in the ball-shaped joysticks that they push and turn. They can duck and weave while standing on a sensor pad and see their movements reflected in the figure of a boxer fighting a computerized opponent. They can put on lightweight helmets and "fly" over virtual mountains and valleys as if they were in hang gliders. Similarly, people in so-called cabin rides at some amusement parks strap themselves into chairs that tilt, shake, and jerk as sounds and graphics on a movie-sized screen take them on simulated roller-

Japanese amusement park visitors enjoy a cabin ride which takes them on a virtual spaceflight. VR lets users safely experience past events, dangerous activities, or imaginary worlds.

coaster journeys through mountain passes, collapsing mine tunnels, or forests full of dinosaurs.

Virtual Communities

Thanks to the Internet, some video games that run on home computers or game consoles, especially the adventure games that descend from fantasy role-playing games, have developed virtual reality in another sense. People who enjoy them have formed networks through which thousands play a game online at once, interacting with one another. For example, a 2003 article states that the online version of the fantasy game *EverQuest* has more than 430,000 subscribers in the United States alone, and more than 140,000 people around the world have played it at the same time.

Online gaming groups are one example of what author Howard Rheingold calls virtual communities. Most virtual communities have been created through online newsgroups, bulletin boards, and chat rooms. These do not involve graphics, let alone virtual reality as it is usually defined. Nonetheless, the people who repeatedly visit such groups come to know each other and often form close (though not always happy) personal relationships, even though they never meet face-to-face and may live in different states or even different countries. Thus, like users of virtual reality, they immerse themselves and interact in a separate world of sorts that exists only inside computers. The Internet becomes the shared "place" where members of virtual communities meet to talk, just as a town square or general store might serve in a real community.

Virtual communities that "met" in particular online environments began appearing in the 1980s, even before the Internet developed. They communicated through computer networks that were the ancestors of the Internet. The first online multiplayer environments, called multiuser dungeons or, later, multiuser dimensions (MUDs), contained only text. As computer graphics improved, the MUDs grew into MOOs (MUDs, object oriented) and MUSEs (multiuser simulated environments), which included graphics.

Building Homes in Cyberspace

Not all online environments centered on games. One of the earliest and most famous, LambdaMOO, was mostly a social gathering place, pictured as a virtual fraternity house. Indeed, LambdaMOO's creator, Pavel Curtis, has said that MUDs and MOOs "created a new kind of social sphere, both like and radically unlike the environments that have existed before."[32] Some online groups that exist today have expanded on this idea to create almost complete alternate worlds. Members of online environments such as There, ActiveWorlds, and Second Life can fly, race vehicles, shop, set up businesses, go on quests, play games, stage parties or other events, chat with one another, and explore dreamlike landscapes. They can claim land and set up homes or other permanent buildings on the virtual ground. Their activities are limited only by their imaginations—and the amount of time and money they can find to spend online. (Members must pay a monthly subscription fee.)

In these nongame worlds as well as in online gaming groups, people represent themselves onscreen as personas called avatars. (The word originally meant the human form of a Hindu god or goddess.) They usually design the avatars to show something about the way they see themselves, who they would like to be, or how they would like others to perceive them. Avatars give people a chance to try out different personalities, including some that would be impossible in the real world. They may have superpowers or be as beautiful as movie stars. They may be of a different gender, age, or even species than the people who create them.

Science fiction writers have been drawn to the idea of computer networks as, in some sense, real places. One of the first was William Gibson, whose 1984 science fiction novel *Neuromancer* introduced a term for such an environment that has become very popular: *cyberspace.* Gibson described cyberspace as "a consensual hallucination experienced daily by billions . . . in every nation. . . . A graphic representation of data abstracted from the banks of every computer in the human system. . . . Lines of light ranged in the non-space of the mind, clusters and constellations of

These cartoonlike figures are VR avatars, each representing a different member of an online community. Avatars may be like or unlike their creators.

data. Like city lights, receding."[33] Movies as well as novels have been set partly or entirely in cyberspace, including *Tron*, *Blade Runner*, *Lawnmower Man*, and the *Matrix* series.

Cyberspace Psychology

John Suler, a professor at Rider University in Lawrenceville, New Jersey, has written a book on the psychology of cyberspace. He says that the "unique psychological features" of cyberspace include

> reduced or altered sensory experience, the opportunity for identity flexibility and anonymity, the equalization of social status, the transcending of spatial boundaries, the stretching and condensation of time, the ability to access numerous relationships, the capacity to record permanent records of one's experience, and the "disinhibition effect" [which makes people feel free to engage in conduct that they might be afraid to try in real life].[34]

These features allow people to create a "second life" in cyberspace that is very different from their real one. They lead some players to take participation in cyberspace beyond art or entertainment, to a level that can have significant effects on their minds. Experts cannot agree, however, on exactly what those effects are. They agree even less on what might happen if in the future, as some writers predict, almost everyone spends large amounts of time in virtual worlds.

Chapter 6

Which World Is Real? The Future of Virtual Reality

Someday, every home may have its own Holodeck. If that happens, how will virtual reality change people's lives?

Most experts think that virtual reality, at least beyond the level shown in today's video and computer games, will not become widespread any time soon. Fully immersive VR technology is still expensive and undependable. Most businesses have not wanted to invest in it. CyberEdge Information Services, a research and marketing firm that covers the industry, stated that virtual reality or visual simulations earned $36.2 billion in 2002, up from $22 billion in 2001. That figure seems large, but it is only a tiny fraction of the amount that the whole computer industry makes.

A Virtual Future

On the other hand, computers are likely to continue growing in speed and in power very quickly, and virtual reality technology will probably improve along with them. Back in 1965, Gordon Moore, a cofounder of Intel Corporation, now a well-known maker of computer chips, proposed what has come to be called Moore's Law, which has often been interpreted to mean that computing power doubles every year or two. In other words, a computer system that costs $1,000 today will do twice as much, twice as fast, as a system that sold for that price about a year and a half ago—or, put another way, a system with the same power as one that cost $1,000 a year or two ago will cost only $500 today. Amazing as it seems, several decades of experience have proved Moore's Law to be true.

It looks likely, then, that by, say, 2015 or 2020, computer systems that deliver convincing, immersive, reasonably reliable virtual reality will cost no more than a big-screen television does now. Most businesses and many homes will have them. Virtual reality entrepreneur John C. Briggs, for one, predicted in the May 2002 issue of *Futurist* magazine that "in the next 10 to 20 years, VR experiences will be fully integrated into real life."[35] Looking farther ahead, Ken Pimental and Kevin Teixeira claimed in

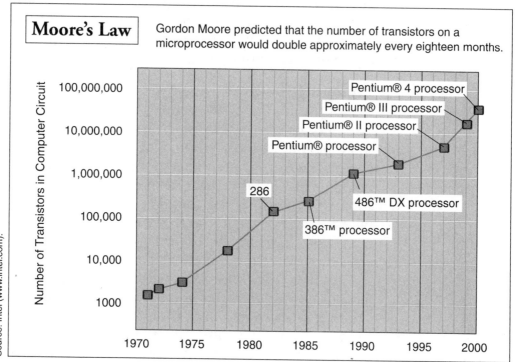

Source: Intel (www.intel.com).

the book *Virtual Marketing: Through the New Looking Glass* that "within one hundred years virtual reality could become a semi-invisible service in society, like telephones, light switches, books, and television—a tool for communication, work, and pleasure that we use without thinking about it."[36]

Some people paint a rosy picture of what life would be like if virtual reality were everywhere. In an article in the journal of the Association for Computing Machinery, multimedia expert Ramesh Jain wrote: "You might experience your friend's wedding in India, seeing what is happening, feeling the warm, humid air of the wedding hall, listening to conversations and the wedding music, and enjoying the taste and aroma of the food being served. You might experience all that and more while sitting at home in Montana on a frigid January morning."[37]

Boosters of virtual reality believe that it will greatly enhance education, science, industry, art, and entertainment, as it has already begun to do. They say it will simplify many tasks and let people express their creativity in new ways.

Changing the Brain

Others think VR may have much less helpful effects. They point to physical and mental problems that some people who use the technology have already experienced. Such problems go far beyond the annoying nausea of simulator sickness. Makers of flight simulators, for instance, found out decades ago that pilots who had used such simulators sometimes made mistakes during actual flying because of differences between the simulated environment and reality. For one thing, simulators cannot mimic the effects of acceleration that a pilot feels during flight. When a pilot experiences these new sensations in the air, confusion results. The problem is temporary, but because of it, pilots are not allowed to fly until they have been away from simulators for at least twenty-four hours.

Some other people have also reported readjustment problems after using virtual reality or doing other intensive work with computers. After researching on the Internet for some time, for example, reporter Chip Brown wrote that he

> woke one night from a peculiar dream, disturbed . . . by . . . the way the scenes had changed; they had not unfolded in a horizontal flow, the movie-like montage of a typical dream presentation, but had scrolled past, rolling up vertically from bottom to top. And my focus had shifted, too, as if the inner observer were no longer located behind my eyes, but had been projected 24 inches forward, out of my body, a displacement roughly equal to the distance between my desk chair and the computer monitor. The conclusion was inescapable. I had become a [computer] mouse. Not even a mouse. A mouse indicator. A cursor.[38]

These temporary effects have made some researchers wonder whether long-term use of virtual reality might cause permanent changes, especially in children, whose brains are still developing and therefore are more easily modified than those of adults. A few even think it might change adults' brains permanently. Psychologist and science writer Richard DeGrandpre, author of *Digitopia*, warns that steady exposure to virtual reality could alter the way people perceive the real world: "Conscious reality changes as the software of everyday life changes, and remains changed thereafter. . . . Chronic exposure to simulated ideas, moods, and images conditions your sensibilities . . . for how the real world should look, how fast it should go, and how you should feel when living in it."[39]

Connection or Isolation?

People also argue about the possible social effects of having most personal interactions occur online, in the virtual or cyberspace world. Supporters of virtual reality and online communities say that future VR and computer technology could change the nature of communication, bringing people around the world closer together.

Even today, some young people who share both physical and virtual communities use Internet-connected cell phones and related devices to keep in constant touch. Some writers, such as the late Michael Dertouzos, professor of computer science at MIT, have thought that most people will share this kind of constant communication in the future. Howard Rheingold has pointed out, however, that such interlinking could be used for either good or harm. It could let massive numbers of people work on projects together or help each other after a disaster, for instance. On the other hand, it could help terrorists coordinate their activities so they could attack many locations at the same time.

A child plays with a virtual playmate who reacts and responds to her actions. Some psychologists are concerned about VR's effects on childhood development.

Supporters also say that the opportunity to lead a "second life" limited only by the imagination can be a great help to people who have little chance to succeed in their everyday life. For instance, John C. Briggs writes:

> VR-enhanced communications will allow those with restricted mobility, confined to their homes, to interact more fully and humanly with the outside world. Because they will use avatars and augmented and assistive technologies on the Internet, they need not reveal to anyone that they have a disability. People with learning disabilities will be able to share their experiences, feelings, and knowledge using communications assistance and augmentation.[40]

People who distrust cyberspace, however, say that withdrawing to an online environment may become a way of avoiding real-life problems rather than trying to solve them. These critics also fear that the chance to represent oneself, and to see others, as beautiful or fantastic avatars could reinforce prejudices against people whose real bodies are less than perfect. Furthermore, a few people use cyberspace disguises for harmful purposes, as when a child molester pretends to be another child or teen in order to lure a potential victim into a face-to-face meeting.

Internet pioneer Clifford Stoll is one prominent commentator who believes that cyberspace society is shallow at best. In *Silicon Snake Oil*, originally published in 1995, he wrote, "Electronic communication is an instantaneous and illusory contact that creates a sense of intimacy without the emotional investment that leads to close friendships."[41] Too much dependence on this kind of communication, he and others fear, can isolate people from real relationships with family and close friends.

Computer Addicts

The isolation is worst for the small number of people who have apparently become addicted to cyberspace gaming. They spend nearly all their time online, ignoring parents, friends, schoolwork, or jobs. They come to regard the imaginary world of the games as more important and more "real" than the world outside. (The problem—or at least the accusation—of addiction is not limited to computer games and online communities. It also occurred with live fantasy role-playing games in the 1970s and 1980s.) A few game addicts have even killed themselves rather than give up the activity.

Supporters of online games and other forms of virtual reality say that the cause of the addiction is the addicts' psychological makeup, not the games themselves. "Computer games bring to the surface the problems of the individual," says Maresa Hecht Orzack, a clinical psychologist who teaches at Harvard Medical School. "Many of these people . . . simply don't want to deal with their everyday lives."[42] If such people did not become hooked on games, these supporters say, they probably would be addicted to something else, such as drugs or gambling. Furthermore, people who favor gaming point out, only a tiny proportion of gamers let their hobby take over their lives. Rider University psychology professor John Suler, for one, claims that the media has greatly exaggerated the reality of Internet addiction.

Suler is one of many experts who feel that the way to keep virtual reality and cyberspace from causing isolation and addiction is to use them as supplements to face-to-face contacts, not replacements for them. He stresses "the importance of bringing together one's online and offline living."[43] Similarly, Joseph Tecce, associate professor of psychology at Boston College, writes, "Virtual reality cannot replace a warm smile, a firm handshake or a reassuring hug. It is essential to connect with someone in [face-to-face] conversation and to share good and bad feelings to ward off loneliness."[44]

Reshaping Social Attitudes

Supporters of realistic online games like *The Sims*, which lets players direct the lives of ordinary people in a virtual city, say that such games can help young people learn that actions have consequences. If a player does not give the Sim characters a chance to eat and sleep, for instance, the characters will become sick and even die. Critics, however, fear that such games could make players think that all consequences are temporary. Real life does not offer the chance to undo a serious mistake by creating a new character or starting a new round of play.

Some writers also say that playing violent, realistic computer games makes people more likely to be violent in real life. A few teenagers in fact have said that games like *Grand Theft Auto* inspired them to hurt or

A computer expo visitor views a scene from the game Doom III. *Debate continues as to whether games like* Doom *inspire real violence.*

kill real people. However, defenders of gaming protest that games do not force people to do anything. The true motivators of violence, they claim, are individuals' psychological troubles, plus problems in society that many people would rather not discuss. As *Computer Gaming World* editor Robert Coffey puts it:

> It's oddly reassuring to be able to point at something you don't understand and blame it for something else you don't understand. Or don't want to devote a whole lot of thought to. It's a lot easier to hold *Doom* [a violent computer game] responsible for some horror than to figure out the role parenting, society, and good old-fashioned unexplainable craziness played.[45]

Are Avatars Human?

These existing arguments about virtual reality's effects on individuals and society are sure to grow more intense if immersive virtual reality environments become commonplace in the future. In addition, widespread virtual reality could raise entirely new ethical questions. For example, it might force people to redefine being human.

In addition to avatars, which stand in for real individuals, artists and businesspeople have created "people" who exist only in the virtual world. Probably the first was a character called Max Headroom, who appeared as part of a British music video program in 1984. Inventor and futurist Ray Kurzweil believes that by 2030, computer-created avatars and characters will become so convincing that no one will be able to tell the difference between real and simulated humans online. Norman I. Badler, professor of computer and information science at the University of Pennsylvania in Philadelphia, similarly predicts that in the future "virtual humans will see with synthetic vision, sense our (and each other's) movements, know us and our actions, and respond in a coordi-

nated and context-appropriate manner. We will communicate with [them] as we communicate with [real] people . . . and use them as information sources, conversational partners, clerks, and complaint departments."[46]

If avatars and artificial characters become increasingly convincing and common, Badler points out, their use will raise "a multitude of copyright and privacy issues."[47] Would one person be allowed to use the form of another as an avatar without obtaining permission? Would famous people such as movie stars, who often sell the right to print images of them, sell the right to use their images as avatars, too? And what if an avatar that looked like, say, a real mayor or senator made racial slurs or other remarks that would harm the reputation of the person

Actor Matt Frewer's actions are translated onscreen into those of his avatar, talk show host Max Headroom. Max was the first virtual celebrity.

supposedly making them? How would people know whether the real person had actually said such things? If someone else had put the words into the avatar's mouth, would this be a criminal act?

Badler believes that ethical issues raised by extremely realistic, complex avatars, gifted with some form of artificial intelligence, could reach far deeper than this. If their programming permits them to make independent decisions, he asks, should they be held responsible for their actions? Could they be punished if, for instance, they deliberately lied to or about someone or cheated someone out of money? At what point would they demand, or deserve, the rights and responsibilities granted to flesh-and-blood human beings?

Withdrawing from Reality

Some thinkers even believe that, for better or worse, constant to virtual exposure reality could completely transform human consciousness. Critics fear that large numbers of people might come to prefer virtual worlds to the real one. Like the philosopher Plato, they would feel that the everyday world is an imperfect reflection of an ideal, but, in opposition to the prisoners in Plato's imaginary cave, they would see the ideal world as the one shown on the screen and the imperfect world as the one outside. Why let others see a flawed real body when online interactions can be delivered through a beautiful, sexy avatar? Why bother with a boring real life when, in an online world, a person can fly through the air, have adventures in distant or imaginary lands, and build a house or even a city in any form he or she wants?

The idea that people might choose to ignore the actual world and withdraw into virtual reality began to concern writers and thinkers long before VR technology actually developed. In *Summa Technologiae*, a book of essays about the future published in 1964, Polish science-fiction writer Stanislaw Lem described an imaginary machine that he called a Phantomat. According to an essay by author John Gray, Lem pictured the dangers of permanent immersion in the Phantomat's virtual reality this way:

> The more realistic the virtual world the machine creates, the more imprisoned we are in our imaginations. As our embodied selves, we interact with a world we know only in part, and which operates independently of our desire. In contrast, the virtual worlds we encounter in the Phantomat are human constructions. Fabricated from our dreams, they are worlds in which nothing can be hurt or destroyed because nothing really exists. In short, they are worlds in which nothing really matters.[48]

Richard DeGrandpre, like Lem, believes that once people become used to virtual worlds, the real world will no longer satisfy them, and they will withdraw from it. This will happen, he thinks, not only because virtual reality will be so appealing, but because social, environmental, and other problems will have made the real world just the opposite. "The ultimate reason we're apt to be taking flight from material reality," he writes, "is to escape the expanding unpleasantness of our inner and outer lives—a melange [mixture] of boredom, restlessness, . . . anxiety, and depression."[49]

Shared Dreams

Other commentators, however, think that the power to share virtual worlds could be a beautiful thing, raising human consciousness to new heights. Jaron Lanier, the man who coined the term *virtual reality*, said in a 2002 inteview that shared online gaming already is "like a technology-enhanced version of shared make-believe. . . . With language, we trade symbols, but with this we trade something beyond symbols. We trade experience." He believes

A viewer sits immersed in a totally virtual environment. Whether VR will make people's lives better or worse remains to be seen.

that future VR technology will "provide a form of intentional, waking-state, shared dreams."[50]

A book and online project about multimedia and virtual reality sponsored by ArtMuseum.net goes even further:

> Interactive multimedia is experiential and sensory, you don't simply observe the object, you are the object. You enter into and become part of the landscape, not just a detached observer. The medium functions as an extension of the self, a reconfiguration of identity, dreams, and memories—blurring the boundaries between self and exterior. . . . The revolutionary nature of multimedia . . . lies in its potential to transform the human spirit.[51]

Notes

Introduction: Walking onto the Holodeck

1. ArtMuseum.net, "Overture: Through the Looking Glass," in Randall Packer, *Multimedia: From Wagner to Virtual Reality*, www.artmuseum.net.
2. Quoted in Steve Ditlea, "Reality Redefined," *Computer Graphics World*, August 2002, p. 39.

Chapter 1:
Airplanes to Arcades: The Development of Virtual Reality

3. Quoted in Edward J. Wegman and Jurgen Symanzik, "Immersive Projection Technology for Visual Data Mining," *Journal of Computational and Graphical Statistics*, March 2002, p. 163.
4. Mark Pesce, *The Playful World: How Technology Is Transforming Our Imagination*. New York: Ballantine Books, 2000, p. 178.
5. Quoted in Mary E. Behr, "Interview: Jaron Lanier, 'Virtual Reality' Inventor," *ExtremeTech.com*, February 11, 2002, p. 1.
6. Quoted in Sean M. Grady, *Virtual Reality: Simulating and Enhancing the World with Computers*. New York: Facts On File, 2003, p. 8.

Chapter 2:
Goggles, Gloves, and CAVEs: The Technology of Virtual Reality

7. Adi Ignatius, "Hands On," *Time International*, June 4, 2001, p. 47.
8. ArtMuseum.net, "Overture: Through the Looking Glass."

Chapter 3:
The Virtual Classroom: Virtual Reality in Training and Education

9. Australian Academy of Science, "Virtual Reality Bytes—Military Uses of VR," *Nova: Science in the News*, March 2002. www.science.org.au.
10. Quoted in Michael Macedonia, "Games Soldiers Play," *IEEE Spectrum Online*, March 2002. www.spectrum.ieee.org.
11. Arlene Weintraub, "High Tech's Future Is in the Toy Chest," *Business Week*, August 26, 2002, p. 124.

12. Australian Academy of Science "Virtual Reality Bytes—Military Uses of VR."

13. *PR Newswire*, "New Generation of Virtual Reality Takes Psychiatrists on the Ride of Their Lives," May 20, 2002, p. 1.

14. Quoted in Clive Thompson, "Can Virtual Reality Improve Your Golf Game?" *Report on Business Magazine*, August 2002, p. 23.

15. Naledi 3D Factory, "Newsroom," www.naledi3d.com.

16. Quoted in Yoav Yair, Rachel Mintz, and Shai Litvak, "3D-Virtual Reality in Science Education: An Implication for Astronomy Teaching," *Journal of Computers in Mathematics and Science Teaching*, Fall 2001, p. 294.

17. Sunrise VR, "Virtual Chicago," http://sunrisevr.com.

18. Sunrise VR, "Virtual Chicago."

19. Quoted in Peter Weiss, "Deep Vision: When Walls Become Doors into Virtual Worlds," *Science News*, June 1, 2002, p. 345.

20. Edwin J. Delattre, "Reality, Unreality, and Virtual Reality," *Arts Education Policy Review*, January 2001, p. 16.

Chapter 4:
Custom-Made Worlds: Virtual Reality in Science and Business

21. ArtMuseum.net, "Overture: Through the Looking Glass."

22. Quoted in Leonard A. Hindus, "Immersive 3D Engineering Environments Are All the RAVE," *Advanced Imaging*, June 2001, p. 57.

23. Quoted in Jim Angelillo and Dennis Neff, "New Visualization Technologies Speed Seismic Interpretation," *World Oil*, March 2001. www.fakespace.com.

24. Quoted in Michael Bramwell, "Escaping Flatland," *Scientific Computing & Instrumentation*, January 2001, p. 26.

25. *Kuwait Times*, "Seminar on 'Vision of Virtual Reality, Surgical Robotics,'" June 5, 2002, p. 1.

26. Quoted in Joanne M. Berger "See Me . . . Feel Me," *Internal Medicine News*, June 15, 2002, p. 47.

27. Quoted in Michelle Mueller, "How Virtual Reality Can Help You," *Current Health 2*, January 2002, p. 16.

28. Quoted in Helen Knight, "Virtual Reality Takes a Leap Forward," *Engineer*, March 8, 2002, p. 12.

29. *Real Estate Weekly*, "Builder Spectrum Skanska Using 'Virtual Reality Tours' to Sell Homes," February 5, 2003, p. 23.

Chapter 5:
Arcades to Avatars: Virtual Reality in Art and Entertainment

30. ArtMuseum.net, "Overture: Through the Looking Glass."
31. Maurice Benayoun, "Far Near (E-motion)," Maurice Benayoun Web site, www.moben.net.
32. ArtMuseum.net, "Pavel Curtis: World Building," in Packer, *Multimedia*, www.artmuseum.net.
33. Quoted in Pesce, *The Playful World*, p. 181.
34. John Suler, "Overview and 'Guided Tour,'" *Psychology of Cyberspace*, 1996. www.rider.edu.

Chapter 6: Which World Is Real? The Future of Virtual Reality

35. John C. Briggs, "Virtual Reality Is Getting Real: Prepare to Meet Your Clone," *Futurist*, May 2002, p. 34.
36. Quoted in Christopher Ryan, "Virtual Reality in Marketing," *Direct Marketing*, April 2001, p. 59.
37. Ramesh Jain, "Digital Experience," *Communications of the ACM*, March 2001, p. 38.
38. Quoted in Richard DeGrandpre, "Great Escape," *Adbusters*, March/April 2001 p. 20.
39. DeGrandpre, "Great Escape," p. 22.
40. Briggs, "Virtual Reality Is Getting Real," p. 38.
41. Clifford Stoll, *Silicon Snake Oil: Second Thoughts on the Information Highway*. New York: Anchor Books, 1996, p. 24.
42. Quoted in Jon Miller, "Caught in the Web," *San Francisco Chronicle*, May 18, 2003, p. D6.
43. Suler, "Overview and 'Guided Tour.'"
44. Quoted in Joanne Hudson, "Virtual Reality's Lonely Lifestyle," *Insight on the News*, May 27, 2002, p. 27.
45. Robert Coffey, "Blamestorming," *Computer Gaming World*, December 2003, p. 200.
46. Norman I. Badler, "Virtual Beings," *Communications of the ACM*, March 2001, p. 33.
47. Badler, "Virtual Beings," p. 33.
48. John Gray, "Faith in Political Action Is Dead: It Is Technology That Expresses the Dream of a Transformed World," *New Statesman*, June 23, 2003, p. 23.
49. DeGrandpre, "Great Escape," p. 30.
50. Quoted in Behr, "Interview: Jaron Lanier."
51. ArtMuseum.net, "Becoming Virtual," in Packer, *Multimedia*, www.artmusuem.net.

Glossary

artificial reality: A form of virtual reality that blends live action with computer graphics and incorporates some features of both head-mounted displays and full-room (CAVE) virtual reality.

augmented reality: A form of virtual reality in which a head-mounted display makes semitransparent pictures or information appear over actual objects.

avatar: A persona, shown in computer graphics, used to represent a user in an online environment.

CAVE: Short for Cave Automatic Virtual Environment, a type of virtual reality display that projects images onto the walls and sometimes onto the ceiling and floor of a small room.

computer-aided design (CAD): A system, first developed in the 1960s, by which an engineer or other designer uses a computer to build a geometric model of a product and perform measurements and analysis on it.

computerized tomography (CT): A form of medical imaging in which a computer combines X-ray pictures taken with a rotating camera to make virtual "slices" through a body, for the purpose of disease identification or research.

cyberspace: A term coined by science-fiction novelist William Gibson in a 1984 novel, *Neuromancer*; used to describe the virtual "place" created inside computer networks, represented by graphics, in which humans can interact.

haptic device: A device that creates a sensation of touch.

head-mounted display (HMD): A feature of a virtual reality system consisting of a helmet or glasses; a computer may send images directly into the device, or the device may change the way the viewer sees images projected on a screen outside the device.

heads-up display: A display in a helmet that projects data onto views of the real world; a forerunner of augmented reality displays.

light pen: A penlike device that interacts with chemicals (phosphors) on the inside of a video screen or computer monitor to send electronic signals to a computer, allowing a user to select or modify objects on the screen.

magnetic resonance imaging (MRI): A form of medical imaging technology that uses the reaction of atomic nuclei to a strong magnetic field to produce detailed, three-dimensional images of the inside of the body.

MOO (MUD, object oriented): A multiuser dimension (MUD) that uses graphics.

MUD: Short for multiuser dungeon or, later, dimension; a shared online environment used for playing games or socializing.

MUSE: Short for multiuser shared environment, a descendant of MUDs and MOOs.

panorama: A view of a scene that extends 360 degrees, as if the viewer stood in the center of the scene and turned in a circle; Web sites containing panorama views through which a user can turn by use of a mouse are considered a simple form of virtual reality.

polarized glasses: Glasses with lenses that admit only waves of light lined up in a particular plane; in polarized glasses used with some virtual reality displays, the lenses are set to different planes, allowing one eye to view one of a pair of overlapping images on a screen and the other eye to view the other image in the pair, creating a single three-dimensional image.

polygon: A geometric shape made up of three or more straight sides; computer graphics are made from polygons.

real time: Time in which an event is recorded, and a computer responds to it, almost as fast as the event occurs.

refresh: To redraw the display on a computer monitor or similar screen; this must be done twenty to thirty times a second.

rendering: The process by which a computer draws graphics.

shutter glasses: Glasses, used with many virtual reality displays, in which the lenses rapidly alternate in becoming opaque; they are synchronized with alternating images on a computer monitor or other screen so that one eye consistently sees one image in a pair and the other eye sees the other image.

simulator sickness: A form of motion sickness, including feelings of dizziness and nausea, that is produced when a simulated environment sends signals to a user that conflict with information from the user's own body.

six degrees of freedom: Movement along three axes (left-right, or X axis; up-down, or Y axis; and forward-backward, or Z axis) and three forms of twisting around each axis (roll, pitch, and yaw).

stereoscope: A nineteenth-century device, usually worn on the head, that showed two similar but not identical images to a viewer such that the viewer's brain combined the two into a single picture that seemed to be three-dimensional.

ultrasound: A type of medical imaging that uses high-frequency sound waves moving through liquid to create pictures of the inside of the body.

virtual community: A group of people who share common interests and meet regularly on the Internet.

virtual reality: An environment created by a computer that is three-dimensional, interactive, immersive, and changes in real time.

For Further Reading

Books

Rusel DeMaria and Johnny L. Wilson, *High Score! The Illustrated History of Electronic Games*. Berkeley, CA: McGraw-Hill/Osborne, 2002. Well-illustrated book recounts the development of video games in the 1980s and 1990s.

Sean M. Grady, *Virtual Reality: Simulating and Enhancing the World with Computers*, 2nd ed. New York: Facts On File, 2003. Provides an overview of the development and technology of virtual reality and the ways VR is being used today.

Mark Pesce, *The Playful World: How Technology Is Transforming Our Imagination*. New York: Ballantine Books, 2000. Explains how three types of toys—interactive "pets" such as the Furby, a Lego robot-building kit, and video games—are related to the cutting-edge scientific fields of artificial intelligence, nanotechnology, and virtual reality.

Howard Rheingold, *The Virtual Community: Homesteading on the Electronic Frontier*. Reading, MA: Addison-Wesley, 1993. Describes the formation of an early virtual community, the WELL, and discusses the nature of communities in cyberspace.

Periodicals

Mary E. Behr, "Interview: Jaron Lanier, 'Virtual Reality' Inventor," *ExtremeTech.com*, February 11, 2002.

John C. Briggs, "Virtual Reality Is Getting Real: Prepare to Meet Your Clone," *Futurist*, May 2002.

Richard DeGrandpre, "Great Escape," *Adbusters*, March/April 2001.

Adi Ignatius, "We Have Contact," *Time International*, June 4, 2001.

Arlene Weintraub, "High Tech's Future Is in the Toy Chest," *Business Week*, August 26, 2002.

Peter Weiss, "Deep Vision: When Walls Become Doors into Virtual Worlds," *Science News*, June 1, 2002.

Internet Sources

William Hunter, "The Dot Eaters," EmuUnlim.com, Lively history of video games and computer games.

NASA, "Virtual Astronaut Program," http://virtualastronaut. jsc.nasa.gov. For students in grades five through eight; provides virtual tour of the space station and related learning activities.

National Library of Medicine, "Visible Human Project," www. nlm.nih.gov. Describes the Visible Human Project, which divides a male and a female human body into extremely small "slices" made with imaging technology, for research and for the study of anatomy; provides samples, including video footage.

Randall Packer, *Multimedia: From Wagner to Virtual Reality*, ArtMuseum.net, Excellent history of multimedia and virtual reality, including profiles of pioneers in the field.

Virtual Reality Society, "History of VR," 1996. www.vrs.org.uk. Time line of events in the development of virtual reality through 1996.

Vivid Group, "The Vivid Group of Interactive Artists," www.vividgroup.com. Shows descriptions and short video clips of virtual reality art installations by Vincent John Vincent and Francis MacDougall.

VR Source, "All Things VR," www.vrsource.org. Includes news, reviews of software, forum postings, links, and more.

Works Consulted

Books

Jeri Fink, *Cyberseduction: Reality in an Age of Psychotechnology*. Amherst, NY: Prometheus Books, 1999. Surveys the ways that humans have tried to escape from reality throughout history and warns against the dangers of withdrawing into virtual worlds designed by people whose ethics may be questionable.

Michael Heim, *Virtual Realism*. New York: Oxford University Press, 1998. Describes the development of virtual reality, particularly in relation to art, and considers its possible impact in the future.

Brad King and John Borland, *Dungeons and Dreamers: The Rise of Computer Game Culture from Geek to Chic*. Berkeley, CA: McGraw-Hill/Osborne, 2003. Explains how the fantasy role-playing games of the 1970s developed into the computer adventure games of today.

Clifford Stoll, *Silicon Snake Oil: Second Thoughts on the Information Highway*. New York: Anchor, 1996. Claims that the Internet is not as influential, nor its effects as positive, as boosters say.

John Tiffin and Nobuyoshi Terashima, eds., *Hyper Reality: Paradigm for the Third Millennium*. New York: Routledge, 2001. Essays consider present and future uses of virtual reality in science, education, and entertainment.

Periodicals

Andrew Richard Albanese, "Cyberspace: The Community Frontier," *Library Journal*, November 15, 2002.

Matt Apuzzo, "The $100,000 Virtual Police Officer," *San Francisco Chronicle*, July 21, 2003.

AScribe Science News Service, "UGA Researcher Develops Virtual Reality Environment to Help Treat Smokers Trying to Quit," July 24, 2003.

Norman I. Badler, "Virtual Beings," *Communications of the ACM*, March 2001.

Joanne M. Berger, "See Me . . . Feel Me," *Internal Medicine News*, June 15, 2002.

Cindy M. Bird, "Phenomenological Realities of 'Quinntown,' Life in a Cyber Community," *Journal of American and Comparative Cultures*, Spring/Summer 2002.

Michael Bramwell, "Escaping Flatland," *Scientific Computing & Instrumentation*, January 2001.

Canadian Corporate News, "Vivid Group Inc. and JesterTek Inc.: Virtual Reality Industry Pioneer Is Given the Lifetime Achievement Award at the 2003 Canada New Media Awards," June 6, 2003.

Canberra Times, "Stylin' Up for a Spin in the Virtual Reality Lane," May 30, 2003.

Robert Coffey, "Blamestorming," *Computer Gaming World*, December 2003.

Ben Delaney, "Enter the Cyber-Utility: Virtual Reality Comes of Age in the Power Industry," *Public Utilities Fortnightly*, July 1, 2003.

Edwin J. Delattre, "Reality, Unreality, and Virtual Reality," *Arts Education Policy Review*, January 2001.

Steve Ditlea, "Reality Redefined," *Computer Graphics World*, August 2002.

Economist, "Curing Vertigo with Virtual Reality," February 10, 2001.

Ben Feller, "More Kids Plugged into Computers," *San Francisco Chronicle*, October 30, 2003.

Paul J. Ford, "Paralysis Lost: Impacts of Virtual Worlds on Those with Paralysis," *Social Theory and Practice*, October 2001.

Andrew Freiburghouse, "Virtual Reality Check," *Forbes*, April 2, 2001.

John Gray, "Faith in Political Action Is Dead: It Is Technology That Expresses the Dream of a Transformed World,'" *New Statesman*, June 23, 2003.

Leonard A. Hindus, "Immersive 3D Engineering Environments Are All the RAVE," *Advanced Imaging*, June 2001.

Joanne Hudson, "Virtual Reality's Lonely Lifestyle," *Insight on the News*, May 27, 2002.

Adi Ignatius, "Hands On," *Time International*, June 4, 2001.

Ramesh Jain, "Digital Experience," *Communications of the ACM*, March 2001.

Lane Jennings, "From Virtual Communities to Smart Mobs," *Futurist*, May/June 2003.

R. Colin Johnson, "'Sympathetic' Haptic Device Feels Every Remote Move," *Electronic Engineering Times*, July 14, 2003.

Matt Kinsman, "Better than the Real Thing," *Promo*, May 1, 2003.

Helen Knight, "Virtual Reality Takes a Leap Forward," *Engineer*, March 8, 2002.

Kuwait Times, "Seminar on 'Vision of Virtual Reality, Surgical Robotics,'" June 5, 2002.

Oh Nam Kwon, "Enhancing Spatial Visualization Through Virtual Reality (VR) on the Web," *Journal of Computers in Mathematics and Science Teaching*, Spring 2002.

Linda Law, "Medicine: The New Frontier for Virtual Reality," *Advanced Imaging*, June 2002.

Jim Louderback, "Real-World Lessons," *USA Weekend*, July 25–27, 2003.

Carlos Martinez, "Phobics Face Virtual Reality to Overcome Their Fears," *San Fernando Valley Business Journal*, April 15, 2002.

Rory McCloy and Robert Stone, "Virtual Reality in Surgery," *British Medical Journal*, October 20, 2001.

Medical Devices & Surgical Technology Week, "Virtual Reality System Provides Effective Hand-Impairment Therapy," February 17, 2002.

Jon Miller, "Caught in the Web," *San Francisco Chronicle*, May 18, 2003.

M2 Presswire, "Research Re-creates Ancient Roman Virtual Reality with 21st Century 3-D Technology," May 20, 2003.

Michelle Mueller, "How Virtual Reality Can Help You," *Current Health* 2, January 2002, p. 16.

Lee J. Nelson, "Stereoscopic Vision: Get into the GRUVE," *Advanced Imaging*, June 2001.

Nottingham Evening Post, "Virtual Reality—It's a Lesson in *Life*," March 25, 2003.

Orlando Business Journal, "Virtual Adventures Alleviate Pain," October 12, 2001.

Poptronics, "Virtual Therapy," November 2001.

Presentations, "In the Boardroom (Virtual Reality)," May 2003.

PR Newswire, "New Generation of Virtual Reality Takes Psychiatrists on the Ride of Their Lives," May 20, 2002.

———, "Students Travel the World Using Digital Tech Frontier's Virtual Reality Educational Tools," April 29, 2003.

Janet Rae-Dupree, "Get in Touch with Your PC," *U.S. News & World Report*, August 6, 2001.

Real Estate Weekly, "Builder Spectrum Skanska Using 'Virtual Reality Tours' to Sell Homes," February 5, 2003.

Giuseppe Riva and Francesco Vincelli, "Virtual Reality as an Advanced Imaginal System," *International Journal of Action Methods*, Summer 2001.

Christopher Ryan, "Virtual Reality in Marketing," *Direct Marketing*, April 2001.

Ralph Schroeder, Avon Huxor, and Andy Smith, "Activeworlds: Geography and Social Interaction in Virtual Reality," *Futures*, September 2001.

Maria T. Schultheis, Jessica Himelstein, and Albert A. Rizzo, "Virtual Reality and Neuropsychology: Updating the Current Tools," *Journal of Head Trauma Rehabilitation*, October 2002.

Science Letter, "New Virtual Reality Array Eliminates Disorienting 3-D Goggles," June 2, 2003.

Carl Sherman, "Virtual Reality Makes Exposure Therapy More Palatable, Effective," *Clinical Psychiatry News*, April 2002.

Bill Siuru, "Virtual Reality Helps Train Those Who Wear Hard Hats," *Poptronics*, October 2002.

Adrian Smith, "Virtual Reality Improves Hazard Awareness," *International Railway Journal*, April 2003.

Michael Snider, "Golf: It Don't Mean a Thing If You Ain't Got That Swing," *Maclean's*, June 16, 2003.

Tracy Staedter, "Haptics: A Glove and Mechanical Assembly Let You Feel the Unreal," *Technology Review*, April 2002.

Jean Thilmany, "Electronic Spelunkers," *Mechanical Engineering-CIME*, June 2001.

Clive Thompson, "Can Virtual Reality Improve Your Golf Game?" *Report on Business Magazine*, August 2002.

Sarah Tilton, "Sniff-N-Scratch: Stop and Smell the Virtual Gunpowder," *Time International*, June 4, 2001.

Edward J. Wegman and Jurgen Symanzik, "Immersive Projection Technology for Visual Data Mining," *Journal of Computational and Graphical Statistics*, March 2002.

Yoav Yair, Rachel Mintz, and Shai Litvak, "3D-Virtual Reality in Science Education: An Implication for Astronomy Teaching," *Journal of Computers in Mathematics and Science Teaching*, Fall 2001.

Heewon Yang and Raymond Poff, "Virtual Reality Therapy," *Parks & Recreation*, May 2001.

Matthew Yi, "Not Your Daddy's PC," *San Francisco Chronicle*, October 20, 2003.

Internet Sources

Jim Angelillo and Dennis Neff, "New Visualization Technologies Speed Seismic Interpretation," *World Oil*, March 2001. www.fakespace.com.

Australian Academy of Science, "Virtual Reality Bytes—Military Uses of VR," *Nova: Science in the News*, March 2002. www.science.org.au.

Maurice Benayoun, "Far Near (E-motion)," www.moben.net.

Brown University Department of Anthropology, "Petra: The Great Temple Excavation," 1999. www.brown.edu.

Contact Consortium, "Upcoming Events," www.ccon.org.

Department of Computer Science, "Effective Virtual Environments," University of North Carolina, Chapel Hill, www.cs.unc.edu.

Digital Tech Frontier, "Virtual Reality Development Lab," www.wecantakeyouthere.com.

Electronic Visualization Laboratory, "Tele-immersion," University of Illinois at Chicago, www.evl.uic.edu.

Louise Elliott, "Immersive Visualization of Virtual Prototypes," *Desk Engineering Online*, February 2003. www.deskeng.com.

Human Interface Technology Laboratory, "Human Interface Technology Laboratory Projects," University of Washington, Seattle, www.hitl.washington.edu.

Kassandra Kania, "Virtual Reality Moves into the Medical Mainstream," *Medical Device and Diagnostic Industry*, May 2000. www.devicelink.com.

Michael Macedonia, "Games Soldiers Play," *IEEE Spectrum Online*, March 2002. www.spectrum.ieee.org.

Musenet, "The Multi-User Science Education Network," http:// guest.musenet.org.

Naledi 3D Factory, "Newsroom," www.naledi3d.com.

Donald E. Parker, "Motion Sickness," Human Interface Technology Laboratory, University of Washington, Seattle, www.hitl.wash ington.edu.

Responsive Environments Group, "Projects," Massachusetts Institute of Technology Media Lab, www.media.mit.edu.

"Rachel's Super MOO List of Educational MOOs," www-vrl. umich.edu.

John Suler, "Internet Addiction in a Nutshell," John Suler Web site, 1999. www.rider.edu.

———, "Overview and 'Guided Tour,'" *Psychology of Cyberspace*, 1996. www.rider.edu.

Sunrise VR, "About Virtual Reality," http://sunrisevr.com.

———, "Virtual Chicago," http://sunrisevr.com.

Tech TV, "'Max Headroom' on TechTV," www.techtv.com.

University of Michigan, "Multidimensional Human Embryo Project," http://embryo.soad.umich.edu.

Virtual Reality Laboratory, "Welcome to the VRL Home Page," University of Michigan, www-vrl.umich.edu.

"VR Art Projects," www.evl.uic.ed.

Index

addiction, to technology or gaming, 86
America's Army (simulation), 38, 39
anatomy, teaching, 43
applications. *See specific types of applications*
archaeological applications, 54
architecture, 46–47, 62–65
ARPAnet, 71, 76
art applications, 66–69
artificial reality, 37
astronomy, 46, 49
Atari, 71–73
augmented reality, 34, 55–56
avatars, 77, 78, 88–90

Badler, Norman I., 88–90
Baer, Ralph, 71
Beck Group, 63–64
Benayoun, Maurice, 69
Berez, Joel, 74
Beyond Zork (game), 74
biological applications, 55
Blank, Marc, 74
boredom, controlling, 60
Bosnia (Holzer and Donovan), 68
Bourdon, Laurent, 54
brain, effects on, 82–83
Briggs, John C., 81, 85
Brooks, Frederick, 19–20, 25
Brown, Chris, 83
Brown University, 54
Bushnell, Nolan, 71–72

CAVE (Cave Automatic Virtual Environment), 34–37, 63, 69
cave drawings, 12

chemistry applications, 52
classroom applications, 45–47
Coffey, Robert, 88
communications
  effects on, 84–85, 86–87
  with users, 28–31
communities, virtual, 76
computers
  development of, 16–17
  learning and, 49–50
  processing power of, 27–28, 80–81
  students and, 46
  see also games
conCAVE, 53
conferences, virtual, 65
costs, of technology, 37, 63
crash tests, 63
Cruz-Neira, Carolina, 34
CubicMouse, 54
Curtis, Pavel, 76–77
CyberEdge Information Services, 80
CyberGrasp, 32, 43
cyberspace, 77–79

Dabney, Ted, 71
Danford, Peter, 48, 49
DataGlove, 23–24
Davies, Char, 66, 67
DeFanti, Thomas, 34, 35
DeGrandpre, Richard, 83, 91
Delattre, Edwin J., 50
Dertouzos, Michael, 84
desensitization therapy, 57–59
design applications, 61–65
DESTINI (Design Estimating Integration Initiative), 64

Picture Credits

About the Author

Lisa Yount earned a bachelor's degree with honors in English and creative writing from Stanford University. She has been a professional writer and editor for thirty-five years, producing educational materials, magazine articles, and more than forty books for young adults and adults. Her books for Lucent include *Gene Therapy*, *History of Medicine*, and *Pirates*. A budding "second career" as an artist using computer graphics led to her interest in virtual reality. She lives in El Cerrito, California, with her husband, a large library, and several cats.